BENAUD IN WISDEN

BENAUD IN WISDEN

Edited by
Rob Smyth

B L O O M S B U R Y
LONDON • NEW DELHI • NEW YORK • SYDNEY

John Wisden & Co Ltd
An imprint of Bloomsbury Publishing Plc

50 Bedford Square
London
WC1B 3DP
UK

1385 Broadway
New York
NY 10018
USA

www.bloomsbury.com

WISDEN and the wood-engraving device are trademarks of
John Wisden & Company Ltd, a subsidiary of Bloomsbury Publishing Plc

First published 2015

www.wisden.com
www.wisdenrecords.com
Follow Wisden on Twitter @WisdenAlmanack and on Facebook at Wisden Sports

British Library Cataloguing-in-Publication Data
A catalogue record for this book is available from the British Library.

Library of Congress Cataloguing-in-Publication data has been applied for.

ISBN: HB: 978-1-4729-2645-6
ePub: 978-1-4729-2644-9

2 4 6 8 10 9 7 5 3 1

Typeset in 10.25pt Minion by Deanta Global Publishing Services, Chennai, India
Printed and bound in Great Britain by CPI Group (UK) Ltd, Croydon CR0 4YY

To find out more about our authors and books visit www.wisden.com.
Here you will find extracts, author interviews, details of forthcoming events
and the option to sign up for our newsletters.

Foreword

Memories live longer than dreams…

The scene is Hamilton Oval in Newcastle, 1945. The dark clouds of Second World War had started to pass and the hot Australian sun was baking down on the players in the annual high-school match between Combined Sydney and Combined Country Northern. A duel was raging between a 14-year-old fair-headed batsman from Sydney and a left-arm orthodox bowler one year older than him, with both treating the match as an important step towards their dream of representing Australia.

The batsman had frustrated the bowler by playing a straight bat throughout his innings and, after watching yet another delivery played dead, the bowler decided to surprise the fair-haired kid with a "chinaman". It was a beauty and, while he dug it out, the look of surprise that danced across the batsman's face would be fondly remembered by the two opponents, who would become close friends over the next 70 years – a time that went all too quickly.

Richie Benaud was the batsman, I was the bowler and that schoolboy match was the forerunner to what would become a lifelong friendship when we met again as teammates in the 1948-49 New South Wales state squad. From close quarters I watched Richie's ascent from an 18-year-old who represented his state to a 21-year-old who was picked for Australia.

It wasn't a dream run. He suffered some painful setbacks along the way, including the time he was hit straight between the eyes when he played an attempted hook shot during a Second XI match between NSW and Victoria and suffered a depressed fracture of the skull. On another occasion he was struck in the mouth by a square cut played by the South African John Waite and, while the aftermath kept the dentist busy, the blow failed to dampen Richie's determination to be the best he possibly could with bat and ball.

He had a burning desire to succeed and he turned net sessions at the Sydney Cricket Ground into the closest thing possible to a match. Before he bowled at training Richie told the batsman the "field" he'd set, and his aim was to restrict them to scoring only two runs per over. He explained the reason he constantly worked on his action and his delivery, and why he treated training with the intensity of a match: he believed the English bowlers were so accurate due to the fact they bowled up to 1,000 overs during a county season. So he attempted to emulate that by bowling unchanged at training for two solid hours.

In those days we cricketers travelled to the SCG by train and tram. I'd meet Richie at Central Station after work and we'd then head to training. We lived along the same train line, so on our way home – while other passengers would read the newspaper, have a nap, look blankly out the window – Richie and I would have great discussions about cricket and how we could improve, and the tactics that could be implemented in the next match. They were enlightened and inspired conversations that allowed me to gain an appreciation for his brilliant leadership and the tactics that would ensure his place among the game's great thinkers and leaders.

Richie's contribution to cricket as a player, captain and commentator has been well documented since his passing on April 10, 2015. My offering here is to commemorate the man – the lifelong friend – who had a profound impact on my life. He was a generous friend who valued honesty; he was rich with his praise when it was deserved; he never shied away from addressing matters that needed to be discussed; and he had a rare dignity.

I know he is regarded by many as having the same kind of impact on the game as Dr W. G. Grace, Sir Jack Hobbs, Sir Don Bradman and the many other great men from all cricket nations whose feats are documented in *Wisden*, the bible of cricket. But as great as he was, the life of Richie Benaud shouldn't simply be summed up by his performances as a cricketer.

The measure of his life is the man he was. I think he provided many people with an insight into that when he was diagnosed with melanoma as a result of not wearing a cap or any sunscreen as a player, because he used his diagnosis to warn people of the dangers of the sun.

I have heard people say that cricket won't ever be the same without Richie and I don't disagree, because I mourn that fair-headed kid I first bowled to all those years ago. He was my Test captain, he was a great man, but first and foremost Richie Benaud was my friend.

Alan Davidson AM MBE
Strathfield, New South Wales

Introduction

In his foreword for *The Wisden Anthology 1978–2006*, Richie Benaud wrote: "*Wisden* tells us everything about the game of cricket, always has." The compliment is easily returned. Few have ever spoken about the game with as much knowledge or authority. Benaud read his first *Wisden* during his first Ashes tour in 1953; his name has appeared in every Almanack since, whether as player, commentator or writer.

One of his essays was a tribute to the great Australian all-rounder Keith Miller in *Wisden 2005*. "Keith Miller's statistics… are maybe those of a very good cricketer, but not a great one," he wrote. "Those who look at them, examine them closely and then give something of a wave of the hand, miss the point in the way that some people now dismiss Victor Trumper. Trumper's batting average is ordinary compared to those who spend vastly more time at the crease, but much less time enthralling, entertaining, bemusing and imprinting themselves on the minds of cricket followers."

Miller's name could easily have been replaced with Benaud's. His Test statistics are excellent – 24.45 with the bat, 27.03 with the ball – but they do not portray the extent of his impact. And they tell almost nothing of his performance as captain from 1958 to 1963, when he resuscitated Australian cricket and cricket itself.

Another reason Benaud's statistics do not tell all is because of the slow start to his career. It took him around six years to establish himself at Test level. His life really started to change during the tour of South Africa in 1957-58 (see page 153), when he produced a series of performances that even Walter Mitty might have deemed far-fetched. In 26 months from the start of that tour, Benaud played 18 Tests: in that time he scored 636 runs at 31.80 and took 108 wickets at 20.27.

He was a riotously entertaining batsman, a marvellous close fielder and a mischievous leg-spinner who was forever setting booby traps for batsmen. Those qualities made him a match-winner, and this is something the statistics do support: in 24 Test wins he averaged 31 with the bat and 18 with the ball. In 13 defeats those averages were 16 and 43. Australia never lost a match in which Benaud scored a century or took a five-for.

They also never lost a Test series when he was captain, which puts him in an exclusive club. He took over when Ian Craig went down with hepatitis in 1958, and revealed depths of tactical flair and human understanding that few realised he had. Australia's first series under Benaud was an unexpected 4–0 rout of an England side stuffed full of all-time greats – May, Cowdrey, Graveney, Bailey, Evans, Laker, Lock, Trueman, Statham – and his team won their next four series too.

Benaud's impact as captain went beyond results. If the former England skipper Mike Brearley has a degree in people – as the former Australian fast bowler Rodney Hogg memorably said – then Benaud had a degree in *the* people. He was the Brendon McCullum of his day – a PR genius who gave Test cricket the kiss of his life with his commitment to attack, though he probably didn't use the phrase "brand of cricket". After the 1961 Ashes, *Wisden* described him as "possibly the most popular captain of any overseas team to come to Great Britain".

He found a like mind in Frank Worrell, West Indies' first black captain; their shared values led to arguably the greatest Test series of all time in 1960-61, which included the first Tied Test. The Frank Worrell Trophy, the prize now on offer every time Australia and West Indies meet, really should be called the Benaud/Worrell Trophy. And he really should have been Sir Richie.

"Captaincy is 90% luck and 10% skill... but, for heaven's sake, don't try it without that little 10%..." wrote Benaud in *On Reflection*. "As far as I know, there has never been a captain labelled as great who has not been lucky. It is the 10% skill which is brought in at that point. The captain who sees an opening and goes straight for the jugular is the one who is drinking champagne at the end of the day.

"The one who muses about it for an over or two before belatedly making the nerve-tingling decision, or taking the incredible gamble, is the one who reads about the next Test series from the comfort of his living-room, sipping from a cold can or an iced glass, according to his habit, and making slightly sarcastic comments on the quality of leadership being displayed by his successor. He had trouble deciding whether to have scrambled or fried eggs with his bacon and is never completely certain in which lane he should be on the motorway."

Nothing reflected Benaud's philosophy quite like the Fourth Test at Manchester in 1961, when he bowled Australia to a famous victory that ensured they would retain the Ashes. England were cruising to victory and a 2–1 lead, with Ted Dexter batting gloriously. The wicketkeeper Wally Grout – who had a not-inconsiderable sum of money on Australia to win the match – chuntered as another Benaud delivery was slapped for four. "Stick with me, Wal," said Benaud, who had just switched to bowling round the wicket to the right-handers, an unusual tactic. "We're going to win this game." Moments later Dexter was caught behind; then the England captain Peter May was bowled round his legs, and Benaud ran through England to win the match. "I have never doubted the man since," said Grout.

Benaud did have doubts, frequently, but like all the great captains he maintained an immaculate veneer of confidence. He was a class act, and a class actor.

His playing career is only half his story – if that. As a leg-spinner he had few peers; as a captain he had even fewer; as a commentator he had none. He was two moves ahead in career terms, planning the next stage long before he had finished as a player: he undertook a BBC training course at the end of the 1956 Ashes in England. His life became an endless summer as he commentated in both Australia and England. He was, as Tim de Lisle wrote in *The Wisden Cricketer* in 2005, "the Bradman of the microphone, not just a master of his craft but its definitive exponent".

It was during that 1956 tour, while watching a black-and-white TV in the Australian dressing-room, that Benaud was struck by the value of brevity. He studied the BBC commentators Dan Maskell (tennis), Peter O'Sullevan (horse racing) and Henry Longhurst (golf) and became increasingly impressed with their less-is-more approach. On the field Benaud, like all self-respecting leg-spinners, bowled with wickets rather than runs in mind; off it, he became a master of economy. A Benaud commentary often meant *no* commentary – he spoke only when he thought he could add value. He saw his role as "adding a caption to the pictures". Few captions were as memorable as the one he added in 1981, when Ian Botham smeared a monstrous six against Australia at Headingley. Many England fans of that generation will never walk past a confectionery stall without smiling inside.

It is said of some great commentators that, when they speak, we listen. With Benaud we also listened when he said nothing; nobody has used silence as effectively. He used it in different ways, too. His love of the pause developed after advice from the Australian Prime Minister Robert Menzies. Benaud became a master of using the pause for both dramatic and humorous effect. He had a tinder-dry wit and the comic timing of a stand-up.

Benaud's mantra – don't say anything unless you can add to the pictures – seemed simple, but was clearly not. "Silence is your greatest weapon," he said, yet these days commentators in all sports choose to go unarmed. In that respect Benaud was increasingly behind the times – and thank goodness for that.

He was also totally impartial, another concept that is in danger of becoming antiquated. Benaud commentated on the final wicket of the two most famous England Ashes wins of the last 50 years, at Headingley in 1981 and Edgbaston in 2005. Each time he unashamedly betrayed his allegiance – but only because his allegiance was to cricket, rather than to Australia or England. "It's all over," he said in 1981 as Bob Willis bowled Ray Bright, "and it is one of the most fantastic victories ever known in Test cricket history."

Benaud was not behind the times in any other sense. He scarcely ever used the phrase "in my day", because every new day was his day. It is human nature to get lost in the moment and carried away; Benaud was able to contextualise events in a way that was thoroughly respectful to both the present and the past. When he did so, we listened. He was, as Matthew Engel wrote in the *Financial Times*, "cricket's revered sage, whose name could be invoked to settle any argument about what had really happened on the field: 'But Richie said…'"

Most of the cricket world was on first-name terms with him. Convention dictates that, in books such as these, you use a person's full name at first mention and then their surname. But it has felt slightly odd typing "Benaud" so many times. He was Richie, our friend.

During his last piece of commentary on British TV, on the last day of the 2005 Ashes, he said: "Thank you for having me. It's been absolutely marvellous for 42 years. I've loved every moment of it and it's been a privilege to go into everyone's living-room throughout that time." He always considered the viewer first; his intense dislike of the phrase "of course" was because it involved "talking down to the people in front of their sets".

He was universally revered yet totally approachable. Ian Smith, the New Zealand commentator, said: "He's probably the nicest guy I've ever met in my life."

This book includes essays from a variety of *Wisden* publications, as well as extracts from the Almanack and reports of Benaud's 63 Test matches. Those match reports have been edited to concentrate on Benaud, but can be found in full on www.wisden.com. There are also a series of articles written by Benaud, including appreciations of Sir Donald Bradman, Shane Warne, Keith Miller, Dennis Lillee and the Chappell brothers. *Benaud in Wisden* is a tribute to cricket's best friend.

Rob Smyth

The Wise Old King

*R*ichie Benaud was first mentioned in Wisden *in 1951, after a promising innings for New South Wales against Victoria. Thereafter he made hundreds of appearances in the Almanack and other* Wisden *publications, as subject and writer. Three of the best tributes to Benaud came from Harry Gee, Gideon Haigh and Tim de Lisle.*

"Benaud is one of very few certifiably unique individuals in cricket history," wrote Haigh. "From time to time one hears mooted 'the next Benaud'; one also knows that this cannot be."

When Benaud came top of a readers' poll to find the dream commentary team in 2005, de Lisle said he was "the Bradman of the microphone, not just a master of his craft but its definitive exponent. He never forgets that the pictures are the thing and that his job is to add to them, not tell us what we can already see. He uses silence like a dot ball. Far from banging on about things being better in his day, he insists Test cricket has been more entertaining than ever in the past two years."

It was pretty good in his day, too, and Benaud's commitment to attacking cricket was one of the main reasons for that. In 1962, after a joyous tour of England, he was named one of Wisden's *Five Cricketers of the Year.*

CRICKETER OF THE YEAR 1962   Harry Gee

If one player, more than any other, has deserved well of cricket for lifting the game out of the doldrums, that man is RICHARD BENAUD. Captain of Australia in four successive and triumphant series to the end of 1961, he has demonstrated to enthusiasts all over the world that the intention to make cricket, particularly Test cricket, attractive and absorbing is every bit as important as skilled technique in batting, bowling and fielding. He has succeeded in his aim to recreate interest in cricket because he loves playing it.

That was, of course, why Benaud junior – to distinguish him from his cricketer father, Louis Richard Benaud – took up the sport which brought him fame as a crusading captain and high commendation as a spin bowler, batsman and close fielder. No wonder that Richie – born Richard at Penrith, 30-odd miles from Sydney, on October 6, 1930 – showed a fondness for cricket at an early age. He had his father, a first-grade player for 20 years with the unique feat to his credit of 20 wickets in a match, as instructor and mentor. Benaud senior, a third-generation Australian of Huguenot extraction, and a schoolteacher, bowled leg-breaks during a long career for the Cumberland club, and so it was natural that he imparted the art of delivering them with the appropriate variations – the googly and top-spinner – to his son.

A small bat and tennis ball, then a bigger bat and hard ball, were the implements used by the eager boy in his form-ative years as a cricketer under his father's expert eye. When the Benaud family after living for a while in Jugiong moved to Sydney, Richie went to Parramatta High School, and here he had his first experience of captaincy. At 16, he followed in his father's footsteps by playing for Cumberland's first-grade team and, eventually, captained them. The New South Wales State selectors, ever on the lookout for rising talent, first picked him when 18 as a batsman, and this was still his primary role when promotion to international status came his way at the age of 21 in the Fifth Test Match against West Indies at Sydney in January 1952.

Thus far, his ambition had been realised, but he had no means of knowing that almost ten years later, against the same country, he would lead Australia in the first Test Match tie in history. Meantime, Richie Benaud came to England in 1953 and 1956, and he also earned representative honours against South Africa, India and Pakistan. His gradually mounting bowling skill was evident on his first two English trips, but he is remembered chiefly during those ventures for the dashing 97 he hit off the England attack in the Second Test at Lord's in 1956.

The 1957-58 tour to South Africa at length established him as an all-rounder of top class, for he took 106 wickets, which surpassed the previous record of 104 by S. F. Barnes, and scored 817 runs including four centuries, two of them in Test matches. Ian Craig led Australia in this series, but the following year slow recovery from illness precluded his choice for the captaincy against England when they toured "Down Under". So Benaud, somewhat to his surprise, but very keen to put his many theories into practice, was appointed to the task of recovering the Ashes which England had held since Len Hutton wrested them from Lindsay Hassett in 1953.

Benaud duly completed his mission and fully justified the selectors' faith in him despite fears that the burden of captaincy might affect his form. His fine bowling, which yielded him 31 wickets for 18.83 runs apiece, proved a major factor in Australia's triumph of winning four Tests and drawing the other. Shrewd and inspiring captaincy transformed an ordinary side into an invincible combination bent on revenge – and gaining it.

Eight Test appearances in India and Pakistan a year later and five more during the memorable visit of West Indies to Australia in 1960-61 – all as captain – brought Benaud's total of caps to 50. In India and Pakistan he excelled by taking 47 wickets (average 20.19) in the Tests and in the ensuing exciting rubber against Frank Worrell's West Indies team he was second in the wicket-taking list with 23 to the evergreen Alan Davidson's 33.

Having with Worrell flung down the gauntlet to those who considered Test matches could only be grim affairs, Benaud consolidated his position as a cavalier captain when he visited England for the third time as a player last summer and helped his men to retain the Ashes.

His inspirational value was graphically demonstrated by the fact that although he missed nearly one-third of the matches – including the Second Test – through shoulder trouble and was handicapped in some others, the Australians won the series 2–1 and maintained an unbeaten record outside the Tests.

When Benaud arrived in England with his team he pledged them to play attractive cricket – winning or losing. He also promised more overs to the hour as an antidote to defensively minded batsmen or bowlers. He promised quicker field-changing and fewer timewasting tactical conferences during play. He and his men did their best to carry out his positive policy, and their faster scoring alone proved a telling reason for the success of the tour. When unable to lead his team, Benaud planned strategy with Neil Harvey, his able and wise vice-captain.

Pain, for which he had injections, did not deaden Benaud's intense desire to conquer on an English visit.

That his playing share was limited to 32 innings for 627 runs and 61 wickets for 23.54 apiece spoke eloquently of his influence and worth in other directions. Nevertheless, his contribution of six wickets for 70 in the second innings of the Fourth Test at Manchester, when the issue of the match and series lay in the balance, was a traditional captain's effort made at a crucial time. He explained the achievements of his side by declaring that they had risen to the occasion, but, modestly, sought no credit for his part in them.

It was a great pity that, because of his shoulder injury, Benaud could not give his admirers last summer other than rare glimpses of his best form, but he had already done enough to make sure of a high place in cricket history. He came with the reputation of being one of the finest close fielders in the world – either at gully or in a silly position – and appreciative of the hazards thus entailed he would never ask a man to take up a dangerous post he would not himself occupy. As a forcing batsman, Benaud, tall and lithe, has always been worth watching. His drives, powerfully hit and beautifully followed through, are strokes of especial joy to those whose day is made if they see a ball sent hurtling over the sightscreen. At Scarborough in 1953 he hit 11 sixes and nine fours while making 135.

Still it is as a bowler that Benaud, in recent years, has touched the heights. An advocate of practice and yet more practice, the erstwhile youngster from the backwoods has long had a bulging quiver of arrows for attack. The leg-break, the googly and the top-spinner have been used most often, and lately Benaud has added the flipper to his armoury. This is a ball, spun out of the finger-tips, which flashes across from off to leg – in effect an off-spinning top-spinner. For his discovery of this unusual and effective delivery, Benaud thanks Bruce Dooland, who perfected it while assisting Nottinghamshire after making his name in Australian cricket.

The urge to trick the batsman has developed in Benaud the ability to evolve many more ways of getting a man out than his four basic deliveries. Changes of pace and flight, with the ball released from different heights, angles and lengths, have combined to make Benaud a perplexing rival for the best of batsmen. He really likes bowling, as it affords him more chance than batting to keep in the thick of a fight he relishes. A fighter, indeed, he has been all through his cricket career, which nearly came to a tragic end almost before it had begun when, as a youngster playing for New South Wales Second XI, he suffered a fractured skull in failing to connect with a hook stroke. Fortunately, he recovered to bring pleasure to cricket followers all over the world and to attain a place among the great players, a distinction earned by his taking of 219 wickets and scoring 1,744 runs in 54 Test matches to the end of 1961. Only three other Australians – Monty Noble, Keith Miller and Ray Lindwall – have scored 1,500 runs and taken 100 wickets in Tests, and Lindwall alone (228) has captured more wickets for Australia.

By profession, Benaud, who is married and has two sons, is a newspaper reporter on the *Sydney Sun*. He writes as well as he plays, and his self-written book *Way of Cricket* will act as a spur to aspiring young players to tread the road which leads to Test fame.

In the first edition of Wisden Cricketers' Almanack Australia, *published in 1998, the editor Gideon Haigh retrospectively named an Australian Cricketer of the Year for every home summer from 1892 to 1997. Benaud was the recipient for the*

1957-58 season, following his stunning all-round performance in South Africa (see page 153).

In 2000, Wisden selected a jury of 100 – including Benaud – and asked them to pick their Five Cricketers of the 20th Century. Benaud was joint 20th in the list with five votes, the same number as George Headley and Kapil Dev. Only five Australians received more votes: Sir Donald Bradman (100 out of 100), Shane Warne (27), Dennis Lillee (19), Bill O'Reilly (10) and Ray Lindwall (6).

RICHIE BENAUD'S FIVE CRICKETERS OF THE 20TH CENTURY

Donald Bradman
"The greatest batsman – lifted Australia in the Depression years. Filled cricket grounds and was a top-class selector and administrator."

Len Hutton
"Changed the face of English cricket when he became the first professional captain."

Bill O'Reilly and Garry Sobers
"Finest of their types as cricketers."

Frank Worrell
"A great man who changed West Indian cricket as the first black captain of his country overseas."

From Wisden 2000

In 2001, Wisden Cricket Monthly *introduced a regular feature called Why They Matter. In the January 2002 edition – 50 years on from Benaud's Test debut – Gideon Haigh profiled "cricket's most admired and pervasive post-war personality".*

THE WISE OLD KING
Gideon Haigh

"Did you ever play cricket for Australia, Mr Benaud?" In his *On Reflection*, Richie Benaud recalls being asked this humbling question by a "fair-haired, angelic little lad of about 12", one of a group of six autograph seekers who accosted him at the SCG "one December evening in 1982".

"Now what do you do?" Benaud writes. "Cry or laugh? I did neither but merely said yes, I had played up to 1963, which was going to be well before he was born. 'Oh,' he said. 'That's great. I thought you were just a television commentator on cricket.'" Autograph in hand, the boy "scampered away with a 'thank you' thrown over his shoulder".

It is a familiar anecdotal scenario: past player confronted by dwindling renown. But the Benaud version is very Benaudesque. There is the amused self-mockery, the precise observation, the authenticating detail: he offers a date, the number of boys and a description of the appearance of his interlocutor, whose age is cautiously approximated.

In his story Benaud indulges the boy's solecism, realising that it arises not merely from youthful innocence but from the fact that "he had never seen me in cricket gear, and knew me only as the man who did the cricket on Channel Nine". Then he segues into several pages of discussion of the changed nature of the cricket audience, ending with a self-disclosing identification. "Some would say a question of that kind showed lack of respect or knowledge. Not a bit of it... what it did was show an inquiring mind, and I'm all in favour of inquiring minds among our young sportsmen. Perhaps that is because I had an inquiring mind when I came into first-class cricket but was not necessarily allowed to exercise it in the same way as young players are now."

I like this passage; droll, reasoned and thoughtful, it tells us much about cricket's most admired and pervasive post-war personality. It is the voice, as Greg Manning phrased it in *Wisden Australia 2000-01*, of commentary's "wise old king". It betrays, too, the difficulty in assessing him: in some respects Benaud's abiding ubiquity in England and Australia inhibits appreciation of the totality of his achievements.

In fact, Benaud would rank among Test cricket's elite leg-spinners and captains if he had never uttered or written a word about the game. His apprenticeship was lengthy – thanks partly to the prolongation of Ian Johnson's career by his tenure as Australian captain – and Benaud's first 27 Tests encompassed only 73 wickets at 28.90 and 868 runs at 28.66.

Then, as Johnnie Moyes put it, came seniority and skipperhood: "Often in life and in cricket we see the man who has true substance in him burst forth into stardom when his walk-on part is changed for one demanding personality and a degree of leadership. I believe that this is what happened to Benaud." In his next 23 Tests Benaud attained the peak of proficiency – 131 wickets at 22.66 and 830 runs at 28.62, until a shoulder injury in May 1961 impaired his effectiveness.

Australia did not lose a series under Benaud's leadership, although he was defined as much by his deportment as by his deeds. Usually bare-headed, and with shirt open as wide as propriety permitted, he was a colourful, communicative antidote to an austere, tight-lipped era. Jack Fingleton likened Benaud to Jean Borotra, the 'Bounding Basque of Biarritz' over whom tennis audiences had swooned in the 1920s.

Wisden settled for describing him as "possibly the most popular captain of any overseas team to come to Great Britain".

One of Benaud's legacies is the demonstrative celebration of wickets and catches, which was a conspicuous aspect of his teams' communal spirit and is today de rigueur. Another is a string of astute, astringent books, including *Way of Cricket* (1960) and *A Tale of Two Tests* (1962), which are among the best books written by a cricketer during his career. "In public relations to benefit the game," Ray Robinson decided, "Benaud was so far ahead of his predecessors that race-glasses would have been needed to see who was at the head of the others."

Benaud's reputation as a gambling captain has probably been overstated. On the contrary he was tirelessly fastidious in his planning, endlessly solicitous of his players and inclusive in his decision-making. Benaud receives less credit than he deserves for intuiting that "11 heads are better than one" where captaincy is concerned; what is commonplace now was not so in his time. In some respects his management model paralleled the "human relations school" in organisational psychology inspired by Douglas McGregor's *The Human Side of Enterprise* (1960). Certainly Benaud's theory that "cricketers are intelligent people and must be treated as such", and his belief in "an elastic but realistic sense of self-discipline", could be transliterations of McGregor to a sporting context.

Ian Meckiff defined Benaud as "a professional in an amateur era", a succinct formulation which may partly explain the ease with which Benaud has assimilated the professional present. For if a quality distinguishes his commentary it is that he calls the game he is watching, not one he once watched or played in. When Simon Katich was awarded his Baggy Green at Headingley in 2001, it was Benaud whom Steve Waugh invited to undertake the duty.

Benaud's progressive attitude to the game's commer-cialisation – sponsorship, TV, the one-day game – may also spring partly from his upbringing. In *On Reflection* he tells how his father Lou, a gifted leg-spinner, had his cricket ambitions curtailed when he was posted to the country as a schoolteacher for 12 years. Benaud describes two vows his father took: "If… there were any sons in his family he would make sure they had a chance [to make a cricket career] and there would be no more schoolteachers in the Benaud family."

At an early stage of his first-class career, Benaud lost his job with an accounting firm which "couldn't afford to pay the £6 a week which would have been my due". He criticised the poor rewards for the cricketers of his time, claiming they were "not substantial enough" and that "some players… made nothing out of tours". He contended as far back as 1960 that "cricket is now a business".

Those views obtained active expression when he aligned with World Series Cricket in 1977 – it "ran alongside my ideas about Australian cricketers currently being paid far too little and having virtually no input into the game in Australia". Benaud's contribution to Kerry Packer's venture, both as consultant and commentator, was inestimable: to the organisation he brought cricket knowhow, to the product he applied a patina of respectability. Changes were wrought in cricket over two years that would have taken decades under the game's existing institutions, and Benaud was essentially their front man.

In lending Packer his reputation Benaud ended up serving his own. John Arlott has been garlanded as the voice of cricket; Benaud is indisputably the face of it, in both hemispheres, over generations. If one was to be critical it may be that Benaud has been too much the apologist for modern cricket, too much the Dr Pangloss. It is, after all, difficult to act as an impartial critic of the entertainment package one is involved in selling.

Professionalism, meanwhile, has not been an unmixed blessing: what is match-fixing but professional sport *in extremis*, the cricketer selling his services to the highest bidder in the sporting free market? Yet Benaud is one of very few certifiably unique individuals in cricket history. From time to time one hears mooted "the next Benaud"; one also knows that this cannot be.

In 2005, The Wisden Cricketer *asked readers to pick their ideal commentary team. The results were not surprising.*

MORNING EVERYONE... Tim de Lisle

As well as 42 laws, cricket has many unwritten rules. England shall drop more catches when playing against Australia. ICC spokesmen shall never concede that any team is unworthy of Test status. And all beauty contests for commentators shall be won by a white-haired old gentleman with a dry wit, a calm demeanour, and a wonderful way with silence.

In England, after this season, Channel 4 retires hurt, Sky cleans up, and there will be no international cricket shown live on terrestrial television for the first time since the Second World War. Sky should be able to assemble the strongest squad of commentators ever seen. So this magazine and Cricinfo held an opinion poll, asking readers to name their dream team. And the runaway first choice, at 74, was Richie Benaud.

An electorate of just under 12,000 makes this probably the largest poll *Wisden* has done: it is six times the size of the *Wisden Cricket Monthly* readers' poll, which ran from 1996 to 2002 and always included a commentator category (no prizes for guessing who always won). This time, Richie received over 10,000 votes, which was 3,000 more than the next man. When he says "Morning everyone," he is merely addressing his fan club. If the cricket world had a president, it would have to be him.

Benaud is the Bradman of the microphone, not just a master of his craft but its definitive exponent. He never forgets that the pictures are the thing and that his job is to add to them, not tell us what we already see. He uses silence like a dot ball. Far from banging on about things being better in his day, he insists Test cricket has been more entertaining than ever in the past two years. And he should know: he has been part of the international scene since 1952, and has attended more Tests than anyone else, alive or dead.

Crisp, succinct and unobtrusive, he is proof that less is more even when it's out of fashion. In a sports culture that increasingly runs on hype, Richie never gets overheated. The poll carries a clear message: we're getting bored of more and saying yes to less.

It often seems that nobody has a bad word for Richie, but the poll asked for comments as well as votes, and there it was, in cold print: a bad word for him. "Richie... too old... sorry... time to retire," wrote Josie Forrest, fearlessly. But she was instantly countered by another young female fan, Jansev Jemal: "Richie Benaud – he's a legend, and I wish he was my grandad." And the men piled in too: "I hope they legalise cloning," wrote Neil Marshall. "I can't watch cricket without him."

... The voters have picked a balanced side, half Sky, half Channel 4, part posh, part populist, two-thirds English but headed by an Australian and a Jamaican [Michael Holding]. Above all, they have voted Benaud...

Brighter Cricket

*R*ichie Benaud's playing career was defined by 12 months in 1960 and 1961. He was captain for the Tied Test against West Indies, which resuscitated Test cricket after a drab decade and started one of the greatest and happiest series of all time, culminating in 500,000 people taking to the streets of Melbourne to say farewell to the West Indian side. That was followed by a famous Ashes triumph in England; it all came down to one magical afternoon at Old Trafford, when Benaud ignored an injured shoulder and desperate personal form to win the Ashes with a flick of the wrist.

The full story of Benaud's playing career is detailed in the season-by-season section at the end of the book (see page 129). This chapter includes essays from 1961 and 1962 Wisdens about the most memorable 12 months of Benaud's career, appraisal of his captaincy ability, and a modern reflection on that Tied Test.

"Timing, indeed, was everything," wrote Christian Ryan in Wisden Asia Cricket in 2005. "Cricket's brightest series coincided with one of its drabbest hours. Sluggish over-rates, stodgy run-rates, throwing, dragging, and an avoid-defeat-at-all-costs grimness were pointing the game towards oblivion. Twelve of the 16 Tests preceding that 1960-61 series had ended *in stupefying stalemates. But this was a new decade, a time of long hair and liberation, and cricket caught on quickly. Benaud and Worrell, two captains astute beyond their years, were unbreakable in their determination to play happy, uncomplicated, risk-laced cricket. And from determination came regeneration."*

The 1960-61 series would ordinarily have been covered in the 1962 Almanack. Such was its impact that it stole a chunk of the 1961 edition as well. The English writer E. M. Wellings, who was at the match, celebrated the two teams "playing in Homeric manner" and described it as "The Greatest Game ever played with a ball".

THE GREATEST TEST MATCH   E. M. Wellings

I was there. I saw it all. That is something that countless thousands would give much to be able to say. For it was The Greatest Test Match, The Greatest Cricket Match and surely The Greatest Game ever played with a ball. Australia v West Indies at Brisbane from December 9 to December 14 was already a great match before it bounded explosively to its amazing climax to produce the only tie in the history of Test cricket.

... We all recognised that this was more than a tied match. It was tied by teams playing in Homeric manner.

... From first to last the spirit of enterprise was in striking contrast to the play in most other recent Tests. Almost coinciding with it a bitter defensive contest was waged by India and Pakistan without ever any prospect of a definite result.

Only two years earlier Brisbane had been the scene of the dullest-ever England–Australia Test... More recently

West Indies and England opposed each other with nothing but negative intentions.

Test cricket had come to a sorry pass. Unpalatable though it is to admit, England developed the tight, restrictive tactics. Having then superior forces, they proved victorious for a time. It is not, therefore, surprising that others followed their lead and, in particular, sought to play England at their own game. Hence the tedium of many recent matches. Now Australia and West Indies have given a new lead, which England can neglect to follow only at the risk of grave loss of prestige.

... Post-mortems on such a match are out of place. I am happily content to have been one of the company of 4,100 who saw the thrilling and inspiring end of this greatest match. It serves as a challenge to all cricketers and calls to them to tackle their matches in the same spirit of sporting enterprise. This was essentially a sporting game, as the crowd recognised when they called for the 22 victors in the cause of cricket to show themselves on the patio of their pavilion.

Also in the 1962 Wisden, *the former Australian opener Jack Fingleton wrote about the state of Australian batsmanship and concluded that the best models for youngsters were Benaud and Alan Davidson, two all-rounders best known for their work with the ball.*

CRICKET ALIVE AGAIN
Jack Fingleton

I am writing this just after the incredible tie between Australia and West Indies in Brisbane. It would be a captious critic, indeed, who saw anything wrong in this rosy dawn of a cricket renascence – as we all hope it will be – but one must be practical, and the request the editor made to me long before this aura of brilliancy was cast over the cricket world here was this: how do the present-day methods of Australian batsmen compare with those of my own era?

... One is pessimistically inclined to wonder whether any decade in Australian cricket history threw up fewer champions than the 1950s. Neil Harvey and Arthur Morris, both capital cricketers, were the product of the 1940s. Each was well entrenched as the 1950s began.

Richie Benaud and Alan Davidson I immediately accept as two all-round cricketers who would have been termed "great" in any period of the game, but it is of specialist batsmen I write particularly and I am forced to the conclusion that although many were chosen, few were found.

... All in all, I could think of no two better Australian models for our young players than Davidson and Benaud. That is, as batsmen.

This might seem very surprising. It indicates, to be true, a paucity of genius; but, in itself, it is a tribute to two very great all-rounders. Davidson's defence in the Tie of Brisbane was impeccable, foot and bat always to the ball. His strokes, too, are ideal. He plays all of them.

Benaud has an odd grip with his top hand. He seems to have exaggerated even Don Bradman's grip with that hand, but Benaud, when attacking, is a delight to watch. He has played some of the greatest innings in cricket history – one at Lord's, one at Scarborough, one at Bradford, one Test innings in the West Indies – and if at times he has disappointed us as a batsman, one has to remember that he either has done or is faced with a terrific job of work as a bowler when he appears in a Test. I expect, however, to see him play some more great Test innings.

... I have high hopes that the flourishing bats of Garry Sobers and his henchmen will inspire a young generation of Australians. I have high hopes, too, that the wind of change which Benaud and Frank Worrell so bravely inspired in Brisbane will blow on to all cricketing countries and disperse that mean, niggardly outlook on Tests which says they must be won at all costs and, if they cannot be won, they must never be lost. Had Benaud and Worrell not put that thought aside there would never have been the Brisbane Tie.

In the September 2005 edition of Wisden Asia Cricket, *the Tied Test was selected as one of 55 turning points in cricket history.*

1960-61   Christian Ryan

The scratchy black-and-white footage crackles with youth and daredevilry and wild, carefree strokeplay. This was a series of extraordinary finishes and extravagant flourishes, two months when cricket danced to a different beat. There was the hypnotic helter-skelter of the Brisbane tie; the unblinking tension of Ken Mackay and Lindsay Kline's last-wicket salvage act in Adelaide; the tremulous twists of Australia's two-wicket triumph in the MCG finale. Amid it all shone Garry Sobers's sun-filled swagger, Wes Hall's brimstone and bluster, Alan Davidson's big-hearted heroics, Norman O'Neill's lithe artistry, Richie Benaud's cool head, Frank Worrell's warm smile, Rohan Kanhai's deft touch and timing...

Timing, indeed, was everything. Cricket's brightest series coincided with one of its drabbest hours. Sluggish over-rates, stodgy run-rates, throwing, dragging, and an avoid-defeat-at-all-costs grimness were pointing the game towards oblivion. Twelve of the 16 Tests preceding that 1960-61 series had ended in stupefying stalemates. But this was a new decade, a time of long hair and liberation, and cricket caught on quickly. Benaud and Worrell, two captains astute beyond their years, were unbreakable in their determination to play happy, uncomplicated, risk-laced cricket. And from determination came regeneration.

"Cricket seems to be in the doldrums all over the world," the South African Board secretary Algy Frames had written to Don Bradman. That letter was dated September 1960. Five months later 500,000 Melburnians clogged the streets to farewell Worrell's West Indians, and the graceful game was great again.

Australia followed the epic series with West Indies by retaining the Ashes in England. After a poor start, the series became a triumph for Benaud. In the 1962 Wisden, *Jack Fingleton reflected on the tour.*

AN ENJOYABLE VISIT TO BRITAIN   Jack Fingleton

---

*"-and, departing, leave behind us
Footprints on the sands of time."*

Henry Longfellow himself departed long before Old Trafford became famous. He died in 1882 (in which year, incidentally, Sir Jack Hobbs was born), but the poet's lines had some significance at Old Trafford on August 1, 1961, when, in the last tumultuous hour of an exciting Test, Richie Benaud pitched into Fred Trueman's footprints and bowled Australia to the telling victory in the series. It was a famous victory for Australia; on the evidence, it was an infamous defeat for England.

... In mid-afternoon, the game was as good as over. England, 150 for one, needed only 106 runs in as many minutes. Back in Australia, with the hour around midnight, most turned off their radios and went to bed, accepting the seemingly inevitable.

Come weal, come woe, no Test side in such a position should ever have lost this game. Ted Dexter, in one of the great attacking innings of the century, was 76. Benaud didn't seem to have a card to play. Just previously, against the clamour of the crowd, he had called for drinks. On a hot day, perspiring bowlers and batsmen do need a drink but this call by Benaud seemed more, possibly, in the nature of an old soldier's trick – hoping that the break in play and concentration might do what his bowlers so obviously couldn't.

It made no difference. Dexter sailed on and Raman Subba Row sewed up his end more securely. All that England wanted was just ten more minutes of Dexter but, hereabouts, Benaud played absolutely his last card in the pack. He came around the stumps to pitch on Trueman's marks at the other end. He had to bowl around the stumps to hit the marks at such an angle that the batsmen were forced to play at the ball. Had he bowled over the stumps, the batsmen need not have played with the bat the ball off the roughage.

Benaud had discussed the possibilities of this move the night before with Ray Lindwall, the old Australian bowling fox. Lindwall thought there was merit in it although I doubt whether either thought there was victory in it. Had Benaud thought so, surely he would have tried it sooner.

Dexter went and Peter May came. Usually so reliable and capable, the English captain immediately perpetrated two palpable errors. A swing to fine leg is always risky. It is doubly risky to a ball coming in off the roughage, but the biggest error May made was in attempting such a stroke without covering up his line of retreat. His legs didn't protect his stumps – he could not have been lbw at such an angle – and over they went. May hadn't scored. Brian Close came to turn himself and everybody else inside out with some vainglorious swishes to fine leg. He hit Benaud almost straight for six but he swished fine again and was out, and then Subba Row fell also. A pall fell over the ground. A game virtually won at 20 minutes to tea was lost by tea and all because Benaud bowled round the stumps to Trueman's marks.

So, then, did Trueman's footprints on the Old Trafford pitch leave their imprint on the sands of cricket time. Thus is history made. A little but an important thing with a man like Benaud about.

… Nothing on the field… surpassed the strength of Benaud's power and influence off it. Here was his greatest victory. His team pulled solidly behind him for the whole of this long tour and this is noteworthy for inevitably, because of man's nature, cliques, caves and cynicisms form from long association. The sight of the same 17 male faces over the breakfast table for nine months in itself often starts bickering, but Benaud, like a good officer, kept his men happy. He was always one of them, never aloof. This was achievement Number One.

… In one particular respect Benaud stood head and shoulders over any international captain I have known. His public-relations work was simply superb. His stated plan of campaign at the beginning, to make every match as inter-esting as he could, had an instant appeal and was in contrast to that of the preceding captain, Ian Johnson, who said he would use county games for Test purposes. In all his appearances on television and in his statements, Benaud said the right and the happy thing. He had a flair for it. The year before, when in England as a journalist, he did a course on television and he considered this of immense value. This tremendous medium of publicity he used to great advantage.

And then there was the way in which he handled the press. He had no favourites. He greeted them all as brothers, as indeed they were professionally. I often smiled at the exodus from the press box when Benaud came from the field. He was always available for questioning and, one surmised, helped many with suggestions for angles and stories. He was cricket's gift to the press. Some of my brethren are notorious for getting grouches off their typewriters at the tour's end but, understandably, this time they had nothing but bouquets for Benaud and his team.

In so many ways, then, Benaud did an unsurpassed job for his team and the game... Benaud was always eager to please. No wonder he was always clapped to the centre of every ground on which he played.

A winning captain must have good fortune and Benaud has had his measure of this, yet it could be claimed that he has encouraged fortune to smile upon him. There was one occasion in Sydney, in a Test against England, when he adopted delaying tactics as rigid and as dubious as any I have seen, but he would prefer to forget this. For the most part, he has thrown out challenges and has always been ready to accept them. On good, true Australian pitches he has gambled to excess by sending England and the West Indians in when he won the toss. He won both matches. His declarations have been sound yet sporting. His on-field captaincy has been markedly sound.

I have written at length upon this facet of Benaud and the tour because I feel they merit it. They have to be known and understood because of the important part they played in making this such a happy tour, such a pleasant one for everybody. I can't recall a single untoward incident… I pity the Australian captain to come after him. In the public-relations sense, Benaud has set him a nigh-impossible task, because the next one is not likely to possess the sound press background that Benaud has.

*The 1961 tour cemented Benaud's status as one of the great captains. In the 1979 Almanack, **Tony Lewis** paid tribute in an essay about captaincy.*

… It comes back to that quality of perception. If ever there was a captain who saw something and then immediately did something about it, it was Richie Benaud. His decision to bowl wrist-spin around the wicket to England's batsmen in the Old Trafford Test match in 1961 was not a new move in the first-class game but brilliantly conceived in the face of England's most talented batting. It was spectacular and perfectly timed: such positive, decisive leadership. In retrospect it looks the obvious gambit, but remember that he could have lost the Test quickly had it misfired or had he decided to do it a few overs later.

I can remember playing under Benaud's leadership for a Commonwealth side against Pakistan in 1968. The second unofficial Test was being waged in front of a massive crowd at Lahore. Our opening bowlers, Ken Shuttleworth and Keith Boyce, took the new ball against the openers, Aftab Gul and Mohammad Ilyas, not the easiest couple to dislodge on their own wickets. Suddenly Benaud stopped the play in mid-over and, with a strong sense of ceremony, shifted every fi elder to the on side for Aftab. All Aftab's runs had come that way, but now, instead of attacking him, Benaud formed a ring of men each saving the single from mid-on to fine leg with one back deep at long leg. Aftab probably did not realise himself how obsessively he played every ball to leg. He was suddenly, pathetically, enmeshed. He failed to score through the vacant off side, got himself thoroughly bogged down and barracked, and eventually succumbed to his own bad temper and departed.

Normal cricket was then resumed. I quote this outrageous and unlikely example of field-placing only to emphasise the need for perception and understanding of the game and the players under your leadership; another Benaud example of conviction followed by swift action. It is too easy to sit back and think about change as an over or two pass by.

The Hemingway
of the Airwaves

L *ike all good leg-spinners, Richie Benaud thought two moves ahead – and not just with the ball in his hand. He was planning for his retirement when he was still at his peak as a player. After the 1956 Ashes tour, when he was 25, Benaud cancelled his holiday and stayed in England to take a three-week training course at the BBC. Four years later he commentated on BBC radio, and soon moved into television. He was a devoted free-to-air man, with Channel Nine in Australia and the BBC and Channel 4 in England.*

The first in-depth Wisden *article on Benaud's commentary was written by E. J. Brack in the April 1986 edition of* Wisden Cricket Monthly.

WELCOME BACK TO BENAUD   E. J. Brack

The first stirrings of spring are in the air and the followers of English cricket can start to look forward to the new season.

... Towering over all aspects of the BBC coverage, of course, is the voice and presence of Richie Benaud. As long as cricket is played there will always be arguments. Most of these arguments, because of their subjective nature, will never be resolved. There can surely be no argument, though, that Benaud is far and away the best television cricket commentator that the world has seen or is likely to see for a very long time.

One hundred per cent Aussie, but not at all Ocker, Benaud has emerged as the ultimate cricket communicator of the TV age. Those of us who watched him play saw it coming, of course. Not until Mike Brearley was there ever a cricketer who could communicate like Benaud. On assuming the captaincy of Australia, he made sure that his players, the public and the media all knew exactly what was happening.

… Allied to the communication skills so evident in Benaud's commentaries is his intimate knowledge of cricket, cricket tactics and cricket psychology. This quality was also there for all to see during his reign as his country's captain. Put in the simplest terms, you don't skipper sides containing such bowlers as Frank Misson, Ron Gaunt, Gordon Rorke, "Slasher" Mackay, Lindsay Kline and Johnny Martin to series victories over powerful combinations from England and West Indies without being a very good captain indeed.

The complementary skills of communication and a sharply analytical cricketing mind were seen working in harness more and more often as Benaud's playing career approached its end. I remember a television interview with Brian Johnston at the end of the 1961 Australian tour in which Benaud simply used the questions as a launching-pad. Fixing that now familiar gaze on the camera lens, he embarked on a series of comprehensive and articulate answers. I watched that interview again last summer during a rain-break in one of the Test matches and it stands the test of time exceedingly well. Indeed aspiring Test captains would do well to watch it and use it as a masterclass.

Benaud the writer was catching the eye around that time too. There were crisp, challenging newspaper articles and two books, *Willow Patterns* and *Spin Me A Spinner*, which were unusual in that they contained not a trace of literary ghostliness. Even now, when we are used to the likes of Mike Brearley, Bob Willis and Peter Roebuck giving us high-class cricket literature from the player's viewpoint, these books would make us sit up and take notice. In their own era they had few rivals.

I always felt there was a Fingletonian quality about Benaud's writing of that period. When he took the next logical step and entered the field of broadcasting as one of the summarisers, I could still see similarities to "Fingo" [Jack Fingleton]. What a pleasure it was in those days to hear the Australian tones of one or other of these gentlemen summing up the state of the game in typical no-nonsense manner. There was never time for humbug but always time for humour.

The transformation to television was inevitable, and Benaud has gone on to carve a unique niche for himself in this sphere. What John Arlott was to cricket on radio, Richie Benaud is to cricket on television. Let us consider some of his qualities. Like all good commentators, he knows when to speak and when to let the action speak for itself. He is brave enough to be wise before the event, unlike most of his colleagues who prefer to purvey their pearls of wisdom armed with the benefit of hindsight.

An example from the momentous summer of 1981 springs to mind. As Ian Botham reached his century at Headingley, Brearley appeared on the balcony and signalled to him. Benaud remarked, "Mike Brearley has just told Botham to stick around. If he sticks around much longer, we'll be starting to wonder what England's bowlers will do on this pitch."

I remember thinking at the time that it sounded fanciful. Now it strikes me as a classic piece of cricket commentary.

Another of Benaud's talents is a knack for producing the apt phrase at the appropriate moment. When Rod Marsh, in the midst of a rare off day at Edgbaston in the 1981 Prudential Trophy, ensnared a streaker who had run on to the playing field, Richie quipped, "That's the first thing Rodney Marsh had caught today." Two months later, in the Old Trafford Test, as Botham began to warm up for his third successive miracle with some scorching off-side boundaries, Benaud again found the right remark. "The ball may be over the ropes," he said, "but the Australians are right on them."

Like all popular TV performers, Benaud has built up a repertoire of catchphrases. There's 'In the air… but *safe!*' and then again there is 'In the air… and *gone!*'

A missed catch is dismissed laconically by "Put it down". The tone of voice here is all important, as it is when someone's stumps go flying and wry Richie sums it up in two telling words: "Bowled him!"

Another little Benaud trick is to call the runs as soon as a batsman plays a stroke. Amazingly, he is rarely wrong. Before the ball has left the square he will say "Four!" or "Good shot for three".

There is also the legendary Benaud self-control. He is almost always able to detach himself from the action, and his impartiality is commendable. Only once to my knowledge has he allowed his emotions anything approaching full rein. That occasion was as recent as last summer [1985] when the sight of Andrew Hilditch, the hook-stroke junkie, launching into his kamikaze routine yet again, was just too much for even Richie to maintain his customary *sang froid*. "Oh dear, oh dear, oh dear," he wailed. It said it all.

When you add a unique voice and a natural authority to the attributes already mentioned, it is not difficult to see why Richie Benaud has reached the pinnacle of popularity with television's cricket-watching public. Such is his popularity that, unlike other participants, his public esteem hardly seemed to be affected by his involvement in the Packer Affair.

I salute "the Aussie Oracle", who is King of the Commentators, and look forward to many more years of pleasure, watching cricket to the suave accompaniment of his inimitable tones.

Benaud stayed with the BBC until the rights were sold to Channel 4 for the 1999 season. Before that, in the August 1998 edition of Wisden Cricket Monthly, *he was interviewed by the BBC cricket correspondent, Jonathan Agnew.*

MORNING, EVERYONE   Jonathan Agnew

The decision by the Government to remove Test matches from the list of protected sporting events, opening up the possibility of cricket being lost to the restricted audience of satellite television, affects every one of us in some way. Whether it is the final push into an electrical superstore to splash out on a dish or, merely, the sad acknowledgment that, unless the ECB acts responsibly, cricket faces a desperate battle for survival, the ruling of Chris Smith, the Minister for Sport, will have an enormous impact on the game. Nowhere will this be more keenly felt than in the BBC TV commentary box. Until a few years ago… Messrs Lewis, Benaud, Gower and Co. lived comfortable existences, safe in the knowledge that Test matches on the box without the catchy *Soul Limbo* theme tune would not… well, just would not be cricket.

So, at this time of potential upheaval, perhaps it is timely that Richie Benaud has just finished his autobiography. Entitled, with a dry wit that is absolutely typical of the man, *Anything but… An Autobiography*, it is the story of a former captain of Australia who, having regained the Ashes, never let them go. He became, possibly, the most informed and respected critic of the game there has ever been and, most certainly, its finest television commentator.

As a result, the impression that Richie Benaud has made on cricket – and the millions of children around the world whose first contact with the sport was through his eyes – has been immense.

... "I started on the radio, here, in 1960," he recalled. "I was on with Johnners and Peter West. The following year I worked on Radio 2UE in Australia and that continued, with people like Ian Chappell and Bill Lawry, until 1990 when commercial radio dropped cricket commentary.

"I suppose, essentially, I am a TV man but I do enjoy radio. You have to make the cricket come alive for people who can't see it and, of course, you have to talk sense. I've got great admiration for radio commentators because the listeners don't have a picture of the ground. Having said that, I believe that television is the most difficult medium of them all, including writing. You can't be on the air for more than half-an-hour at a time because your concentration begins to flag – rather like batting or bowling."

Benaud's television career began in 1956 when he was touring England with Ian Johnson's team. "I started to do some work on the TV, enjoyed it, and made some enquiries about going on a course to help me learn more about it. Finally, the only way I could get on one was to miss the holiday we had planned between the tour of England and moving on to Pakistan. Instead I worked from 11am until midnight for three weeks doing everything: football at Wembley, going to the races with Peter O'Sullevan, and listening to a lot of golf commentary before flying on to Pakistan where we were bowled out for 80! But I had learned a lot!

"When I became captain of Australia I began to be interviewed regularly and, in 1963, the BBC asked me to come over as their 'independent' commentator. That was a terrific opportunity because from that moment I was trained by the BBC to be neutral."

Unlike some of his rather more verbose counterparts worldwide (especially on Channel Nine and Sky), Richie – more than anyone – has mastered the art of speaking only when it is absolutely necessary. In my brief outings for BBC TV I have quickly become aware just how difficult that is. There you sit, clutching a microphone in your hand, feeling that you simply have to open your mouth and say something.

"You must only speak when you can actually add something to the picture," Richie explained in a manner that suggested that even in conversation he selects his words very carefully. "I learned that from listening to Dan Maskell on tennis and Henry Longhurst on golf. I loved English at school and, because of my father's influence, I was always a voracious reader as a kid. We used to have our family holidays in northern New South Wales and would play all kinds of games involving spelling and mental arithmetic in the car. Daphne, my wife [who used to be E. W. Swanton's secretary], is also very good at vocabulary and sentence construction."

What about commercial TV? Surely that puts you under pressure to speak more?

"The adverts do make a difference," Richie agreed. "Sometimes on Channel Nine we cut out the ads at the end of an over if there is an important slow-motion replay to show or an incident to discuss. Generally, though, I am sure I speak more on Channel Nine than on the BBC because you don't have the chance between overs."

Chances are, whenever you stick your nose into the BBC commentary box, that Richie will have his head buried in his laptop computer, gently tapping out his latest match report.

Not all 67-year-olds have taken to modern technology so easily, but Richie has an interest in the innovations that continue to increase the capacity – and the challenge – of television.

"I like computers, but I'm not great at them," Richie admitted. "I reckon a nine-year-old child would be better than me, but they are wonderful things. Daphne carries one with her all the time so we are constantly in touch and they are tremendously beneficial.

"The other day Channel Nine emailed to me 15 graphics they are going to use for the next Australian season. I was able to check and send them back. I love the advances made by television. Last summer I had a discussion about 'spin vision' cameras with Geoff Boycott. He reckons they will kill the wrist-spinners because batsmen can sit and study the replays to learn how to read each delivery. I disagreed. I know if I were being studied by a batsman I would scramble the seam so he couldn't see it.

"But many of the new ideas aren't original, you know. I was covering a match in Brisbane a couple of years ago as part of Allan Border's benefit year, in which the umpires had cameras in their hats and the players were all miked-up so we could talk to them. A fellow came up to me afterwards and said: 'That was absolutely brilliant. You must be so proud to be involved with such a modern venture.'

"In fact, I had done the same thing in England in 1963 – more than 30 years earlier. Brian Johnston was in the commentary box, Denis Compton and I wore microphones, and I would tell Johnners what I was about to bowl at Denis. Sometimes Denis could hear me and sometimes not. Similarly, Denis would nominate his shot to viewers, in advance, without me knowing. It was great fun, but maybe it shows that while technology has changed, the ideas are still the same."

The remarkable paradox in Richie's professional life is that, while he has happily commentated on the game from the lofty position of the BBC TV box, he has managed, also, to work for that most thrusting of tabloids: the *News of the World*. It must be a precarious balancing act!

"I started for the *News of the World* in 1960 so I reckon I must be their longest-serving employee," he said, with no small measure of pride. "I've had remarkably few sports editors in that time and have never been under any awkward pressure: I say what I want. If they have ever needed to make changes to my copy, they have always contacted me first and either I have said yes or no.

"The style of the newspapers has changed enormously in that time. The best example of that I can give you is that when I was first made captain of Australia, I invited all the members of the media into the dressing-room for a beer. There's no way I would do that these days – there are so many of them for one thing. The rule in 1958 was that the journalists could talk to the cricketers but if any of the players got into trouble as a result, all the access would stop. We were never let down once. Sadly, the players have to be much more careful now."

… It was time for the killer question. No point in beating about the bush… deep breath… "When will you know you're past it, Richie?"

Surprisingly, he did not even twitch. "I've taken precautions," he said. "The danger time is when you make a mistake and don't realise it. I've got some people lined up who I trust and they'll tell me when it's time to go. Daphne's one of them, but I've got no plans to retire yet."

… As I thanked Richie for his time, I realised I had omitted to ask what must surely be the most obvious question of all: what's his advice to budding young commentators?

"Don't copy anyone. Concentrate fiercely. Listen to as much television commentary as you can and sort out what you like and what you don't. Above all, don't take yourself too seriously!"

Benaud was in the unique position of commentating throughout both the English and Australian summers. His influence at Channel Nine was discussed in the 2000-01 edition of Wisden Cricketers' Almanack Australia.

STILL THE ONE   Greg Manning

... Asked what comes to mind when they think of the cricket on Channel Nine, most viewers would probably not talk of technology, but of the commentary team. Again it is worth recalling the world before 1977.

Cricket commentary evolved on the ABC on radio, where a staff reporter described the ball-by-ball play and an old cricketer commented during the breaks. The great pairs – Vic Richardson and Arthur Gilligan, Alan McGilvray and Lindsay Hassett – were exceptions. For the most part the ball-by-ball caller was an ABC staffer, and when they put the cricket on television the ABC transferred the radio commentary set-up to TV. This was a tactical error. On television we didn't need someone to tell us what we could see for ourselves, and without material the staffers tended to blather, to talk trivia, to whinge about dull play. They betrayed the truth that they watched the game like us, as visitors, from the outside.

What Dashiell Hammett did with murder, Kerry Packer did with cricket: he gave it back to the people who were good at it. Between them, R. Benaud, I. M. Chappell, A. W. Greig and W. M. Lawry, the perennial core of the team, boast 265 Tests, over 400 wickets and more than 16,000 runs. Each one was captain of his country. They bring us a Test match from the viewpoint of one of the cricket family, an insider. So, where an ABC voice used to read a player's statistics, the Nine team let you do that for yourself while they tell you what the numbers mean: "His average has slipped to 35, he won't be happy with that, he needs to convert more of those fifties into hundreds. There are a few good players looking for his spot, but he knows that, he's a fine cricketer." Nothing surprising, maybe, but it's the way cricketers think. And when Richie or Tony reads the line chart showing relative scoring-rates in one-day games, or when they decode the bar graphs that sum up a player's career, they know what these things *mean,* not just how they read.

This is television commentary as a service. But commercial television is not just a service. It is an industry, there to make money, which it does by carrying advertising. As a result, cricket on Nine is constantly interrupted, most often by end-of-over commercials (which regularly consume the first ball of the new over), but also by continuous in-house merchandising of autobiographies, framed photos, bats and statuettes, and by sponsored diversions such as classic catches and trivia contests. As in a good movie, every cut to a commercial break reminds us all, at some level, of the transcendent power of the television industry. To keep the value in its ads, Channel Nine has to advertise itself, and this requires that the commentary team do more than call the cricket: that they play up that aspect of themselves that commercial TV can sell as "personality". So Richie is the wise old king (it's striking how closely he now fills the place once occupied by Alan McGilvray – *plus ça change*); Ian is Mr Spock, the cool technical second-in-command, analysing all, adjusting the field, changing the bowling, probing for weaknesses; and Tony and Bill do the comedy. Tony is the gadget man, and mischief-maker, barracking for the opposition and teasing Bill; and Bill is us. Us with 5,000 Test runs and 13 centuries, of course, but still the cricket tragic, waiting for every ball with the same guileless intensity he brought to the last one, forever the kid at the cricket. The archetypes are familiar.

Benaud's position in commentary boxes in both hemispheres – not to mention his experience as a player – made him a prime candidate when, for the 2003 Almanack, the editor Tim de Lisle decided to find out who had watched the most Test cricket.

BEING THERE   Tim de Lisle

If you want to know who has played the most Tests, the answer is easily found... But what if you were wondering who has seen the most Tests?

We decided to work it out. Given the inflation in the international game, it was probably someone involved in a professional capacity over the past 30 years. We decided not to count watching on television, nor any Tests but official ones between male teams. During the winter, while professional cricket-watchers were scattered around the world, we fired off emails to a few likely suspects. Some didn't fancy the idea; others were too busy – watching cricket. But enough were intrigued for answers to trickle in.

... The same three names kept coming up: Richie Benaud, 72, a fine player who has been commentating ever since, in England and Australia, in one never-ending summer; E. W. (Jim) Swanton, whose cricket-writing career ran from the 1930s to his death, aged 92, in 2000; and John Woodcock, 76, today's elder statesman of cricket writing, who was *The Times* correspondent from 1954 to 1987 and still pops up there, radiating genial authority.

... Richie Benaud, naturally, was in the commentary box, in Melbourne, for the Australia–England one-day finals. We sent a message via Ian Healy. For a couple of weeks, there was silence: Richie's signature tune.

One morning, an email landed – "From: Richie Benaud". It was like getting a postcard from the Pope. "Sorry to be so long coming back to you, but it has all been slightly hectic out here." He had a figure, but needed to check it when he was back home in Sydney. "Cheers, Richie."

Next morning, another email. "I hope the following might fit in with what you want, and I hope I've got the figures right…"

He had totted them all up, scrupulously: 63 Tests as a player, three as twelfth man, one on tour that he didn't play in (Lord's, 1961), one at the MCG in 1963-64, when he had broken a finger and covered it for the *Sydney Sun*… "68 in my playing time, 11 covered in the West Indies, 8 in South Africa, 5 in New Zealand, 223 in England, 171 in Australia, 0 in India, 0 in Pakistan, 0 in Sri Lanka, 0 in Zimbabwe, 0 in Bangladesh." He listed all the ducks as if he planned on breaking them.

In Australia and England together, he had seen 394 Tests, out of 733: more than half. His grand total was 486, a phenomenal figure. There had been 1,636 Tests in history, and Richie had been there for nearly a third of them, weighing his silences, composing his understatements, keeping his cool, distilling all that experience…

It made you wonder how he had sprung so swiftly from the top of one tree to the top of the next. Anticipating this, he had added an informal CV. "Did a three-week BBC television course devised for me by Tom Sloan at the end of the 1956 tour of England, then joined the team in Rome to fly to Pakistan and India for four Tests. On return to Australia, started as a journalist on Police Rounds and Sports at the *Sydney Sun*.

"Covered the five 1960 Tests E v SA for BBC Radio whilst still an Australian player. Captained the side to England in 1961, and BBC TV asked me back to cover E v WI 1963. Retired from cricket after the 1963-64 series A v SA. Didn't cover E v P and I in 1971. Didn't cover Tests during World Series Cricket [which he helped set up]. I watched Tests at the SCG 1946-47 to 1951-52, but haven't counted them as I was playing club cricket on the Saturdays and then was in the NSW team on tour.

… We had asked Benaud to name a favourite Test. "Three of them from different points of view." His reasons are in the panel on pages 44-6.

One last question. When was his first glimpse of Test cricket? "1946-47, Sydney, Second [Ashes] Test. Great disappointment, Lindwall had chickenpox, but Ian Johnson

---

RICHIE BENAUD'S FAVOURITE TESTS …

From a personal point of view: England v Australia, Old Trafford, 1961. "Otherwise life might have been very different." Bowling his leg-breaks round the wicket into the rough, he took five for 12 off 25 balls on the last afternoon, to turn the match and help regain the Ashes.

As a game: Australia v West Indies, Brisbane, 1960-61 – the Tied Test. "Frank Worrell was at Sydney airport on his way to Perth to join his team. He had been delayed by a seafood allergy and Alan Barnes, the board secretary, phoned me at the *Sun* to say his plane was about to land and perhaps I might want to interview him. We had a good chat and as he was turning to walk to the plane I said, 'I hope it's a great series.' He came back, smiled and replied, 'Well, we'll have a lot of fun anyway.'

"Then there was the matter of Bradman asking permission to speak at our team meeting the night before the game. I checked with the players and told him that was fine. His was a very short address, but

---

of extreme importance and unique in Australian cricket. It was a personal message to the effect that we had the chance to make this one of the greatest summers in Australian history, after some ordinary ones. He and his co-selectors, Jack Ryder and Dudley Seddon, would look in kindly fashion on players who had as their priority the entertainment of the people paying at the turnstiles. And in less kindly fashion on those who didn't.

"This fitted in with our pre-series planning, but it was comforting to know that the selectors were thinking that way, and by the time the motorcade farewell had taken place in Melbourne after the final Test, the face of cricket had been changed forever in Australia."

From the commentary box: England v Australia, Headingley, 1981. "The sheer drama of it all. Botham sacked, Brearley recalled, England following on and then winning, booking out of their hotel a day early, Ladbrokes' 500-1, England 221 for their last three wickets, Botham's 149, Willis eight for 43. A commentator's dream match for Jim Laker and me."

... and his tips for aspiring commentators

"Everyone should develop a distinctive style, but a few pieces of advice might be:

Put your brain into gear before opening your mouth.
Never say 'we' if referring to a team.
Discipline is essential; fierce concentration is needed at all times.

(Continued)

"Then try to avoid allowing past your lips: *'Of course'*... *'As you can see on the screen'*... *'You know...'* or *'I tell you what'*. *'That's a tragedy...'* or *'a disaster...'*. (The Titanic was a tragedy, the Ethiopian drought a disaster, but neither bears any relation to a dropped catch.)

"Above all: when commentating, don't take yourself too seriously, and have fun."

From Wisden 2003

and Colin McCool were there, taking nine of the ten wickets. Australia were 159 for four when Bradman, injured and ill, came out at No. 6 and put on 400 with Barnes. McCool took another five wickets to reinforce the thought that leg-spinners were great. I had just turned 16. Over 40,000 spectators the first three days." Australia won by an innings, but Benaud's recollection skips that to focus on the fans. He always was on our side.

A year later Benaud picked his all-time XI for a special DVD, a choice reviewed in the October 2004 edition of Wisden Asia Cricket.

THE POPE'S PICKS   Andrew Miller

Richie Benaud has turned the considered opinion into an art form – the longer the silence, the more apt the *mot juste* turns out to be. And so it goes without saying that after considering for more than half a century his opinion of the greatest players the game has ever seen, the upshot is an all-time XI of typically succinct precision.

The beauty of Benaud's XI is in its balance. Individually other players may have been greater or more crowd-pleasing, but collectively his final pick is seamless. A fire-and-ice opening pairing of Jack Hobbs and Sunil Gavaskar; the incomparable Don Bradman at No. 3; a middle order of Viv Richards and Sachin Tendulkar, who, with utterly contrasting but entirely complementary demeanours, bestrode their respective decades.

There follows a triumvirate of all-rounders at Nos 6, 7 and 8 – Garry Sobers, Imran Khan and Adam Gilchrist – who would put the fear of God into any attack in the world. And to complete the set, Benaud plumps for Shane Warne, Dennis Lillee and a definite googly in Sydney Barnes at No. 11 – thrown in, one suspects, on account of the tightness of the top ten.

There are oddities and omissions (no Muttiah Muralitharan, for instance, nor any of the great West Indian fast bowlers), but just to show that he has left nothing to chance, Benaud even names a twelfth man – his great friend and team-mate Keith Miller – and a manager, Frank Worrell, Benaud's opposite number on the legendary tour of 1960-61, and perhaps the greatest diplomat the game has known. The gauntlet has been laid. Beat that if you can.

Benaud's Greatest XI: Hobbs, Gavaskar, Bradman, Richards, Tendulkar, Sobers, Imran, Gilchrist, Warne, Lillee, Barnes.

Benaud commentated for the final time in England during the 2005 Ashes, the last series shown on the free-to-air Channel 4. In the November 2005 edition of The Wisden Cricketer, ***Emma John*** *witnessed the final, emotional moments of their coverage.*

… Ask him [Simon Hughes] the best thing about working for C4 and his reply is unhesitating. "Richie. I love his enthusiasm. Anything I do he always says something encouraging." As C4's fledglings have found their feathers, it is Richie who has helped groom them. "I think most of us follow the Benaud school of commentary," agrees [Mike] Atherton, "which is to keep your mouth shut unless you've got something to add to the pictures."

It is not just the commentators who pay their tributes to the abdicating king of commentary. Shane Warne jogs over to the box to shake Richie's hand, and at tea on the final day the crowd salute him so wildly that he is forced to give a quasi-royal appearance at the front of the commentary box.

Benaud's departure from British screens was covered in Wisden 2006 *as part of an essay about the media coverage of the Ashes.*

ALL HAIL! Quentin Letts

… There was a sense of it all getting worse. Summer 2005 was Richie Benaud's last in England as a television commentator. Benaud's skills at the microphone were discussed during numerous tributes, colleagues such as Mark Nicholas praising his economy, professionalism and lack of bias. A typical Benaud touch came after Ian Bell had dropped a catch. By the end of that over Channel 4 had assembled a package which showed how today's fielders invariably react after they have fluffed a sitter. They clap their hands and shout at their team-mates to try harder. Bell had done just the same thing. Benaud

EVENING, EVERYONE

With Channel 4 losing their cricket rights, the Oval Test was Richie Benaud's last as a commentator in England after 42 years:

"Morning, everyone."
Benaud's catchphrase

"Calm, unhurried, courteous, literate, professional: those were Benaud's trademarks, and they seemed right for cricket. Now, cricket, like everything else in life, is faster, ruder and cruder. His quiet, precise voice belongs to an age when a cover-driven boundary was always applauded, no matter which side had hit it."
Leader, The Observer

"In many ways Richie has been the Hemingway of the airwaves, treating us to an economy of words and style... Often, he leaves things partially unsaid, which is inclusive for the viewers as it makes them work just that little bit harder."
Mike Atherton

"I carry a lot of music around with me, and one of the great ones for me is Andrea Bocelli and Sarah Brightman singing that wonderful duet, *Time To Say Goodbye*. And that's what it is, as far as I'm concerned – time to say goodbye. And add to that, thank you for having me. It's been absolutely marvellous for 42 years. I've loved every moment of

(Continued)

it and it's been a privilege to go into everyone's living-room throughout that time. What's even better is that it's been a great deal of fun. [At which point Kevin Pietersen is bowled by Glenn McGrath for 158.] But not so for the batsman – McGrath has picked him off… And in the commentary box now, Mark Nicholas and Tony Greig."
Benaud's sign-off

"The Bradman of the commentary box."
Mark Nicholas

"He has a genius for not stating the blindingly obvious."
Leader, the Daily Telegraph

"Daphne's seen the show 32 times, and I've seen it 26 times."
Benaud on the family enthusiasm for the musical Cats

"Dreaded foe of mawkish sentiment, laureate of laconic austerity… Richie in the dress circle, Maltesers on lap, mouthing 'Macavity's a mystery cat, he's called the hidden paw' along with the cast – whether the image is more or less incongruous than finding Lady Thatcher in the next booth at an erotic club one night in Bangkok is an intriguing point of academic debate."
Matthew Norman, the Sunday Telegraph

From Wisden 2006

wondered gently if perhaps Bell's team-mates might be justified in telling him that he, not they, was the one who should try harder.

Despite all Benaud's excellence, no one emulated the old boy. Television's new generation of cricket commentators have not made themselves irreplaceable.

The 2006 Almanack also included an essay on cricket and the internet, part of which served to highlight Benaud's enduring generosity of spirit.

LIKE FALLING OFF A BLOG   Alastair McLellan

… Among all the chatter, perhaps the real blog treasures are the previously untold tales throwing new light on the game's legends. Over to the former Lancashire left-arm spinner, Alex Barnett, and his fond farewell to Richie Benaud.

"It was the 1993 B&H semi-final against Leicestershire. I delivered a dreadful long-hop which the batsman tried to hit into Manchester. But he swung so hard he missed. The next day I watched a recording of the BBC's coverage, and the great man was in the commentary box as I bowled my filthy half-tracker. I listened closely to hear how one of the world's greatest sporting commentators might describe one of the world's worst deliveries.

"As it happened the ball just missed the off stick. Then Richie chimed in: 'Ah, that'll be the skidder, where he releases the ball a bit quicker, undercuts so the seam doesn't touch the wicket and the ball goes straight on.'

"Thanks, Richie, I am for ever indebted."

Benaud also wrote for the News of the World *for 50 years, and was involved in the spot-fixing exclusive during the Pakistan tour of England in 2010. In the October 2010 edition of* The Wisden Cricketer, *Sam Peters gave a personal account of his and Benaud's role on one of cricket's darker days.*

AT THE EYE OF THE STORM   Sam Peters

I had just finished eating my lunch at Lord's when my sports editor's name, Paul McCarthy, flashed up on my mobile phone. Working for the *News of the World,* when it's Saturday afternoon and your boss calls, you answer.

"Sam, pack up your gear and get in a taxi to Wapping, now," McCarthy said. "You've got a meeting with the editor in an hour. Don't tell anyone where or what you're doing, just come straight away. And bring Richie." Richie is, of course, Richie Benaud, the *News of the World*'s cricket columnist of 50 years and the man whose voice is synonymous with the game.

"Richie, we've got to leave," I whispered in the great man's ear. "Why?" was his perfectly reasonable response. "The editor wants to see us immediately. I can't tell you anything else."

"OK, but I need to ring Daphne," he said before carefully inputting his wife's number, which is written in pen on the back, into his phone. I made some excuses to my fellow hacks before slipping out down the stairs of the media centre, having told Richie I'd meet him at the North Gate.

I hailed a cab and ushered Richie in. "Richie, I think I know what…" I started to say. I turned and saw him with one finger pressed to his lips with another pointing in the direction of the cabbie. The great man was more switched on than I was. I punched a few words into my phone and showed him the screen so as not to alert the cabbie. "This has to be match-fixing," it read. Richie nodded solemnly in agreement.

The taxi ride across London went by in a blur. I passed the time by quizzing Richie who he admired most in the media during all his time in sport (horse racing's Sir Peter O'Sullevan, for the record) but my mind was buzzing…

Cricket lost its voice on April 10, 2015, when Benaud passed away after suffering from skin cancer. The Wisden India *website paid tribute to "one of a kind".*

THE LILTING MORSE CODE OF RICHIE BENAUD

Dileep Premachandran

I was half a world away from the Melbourne Cricket Ground, and didn't even see the game live. All that cricket fans in England saw of the World Championship of Cricket in March 1985 was a half-hour highlights package put together by Channel Nine. Yet, all these years later, I remember incidents from that final better than I do matches that I watched from the press box a couple of years ago.

The main reason for that is a snippet of commentary. Qasim Omar had made an unbeaten 42 in Pakistan's semifinal win against West Indies, and when he walked out to bat in the final with his side 29 for 2, the match was finely poised. Kapil Dev's first ball to him was full and swung in. To appreciate what a great delivery it was, you needed to listen to Richie Benaud up in the commentary box.

Even in an age of understated game-callers, Benaud was a minimalist. Not for him shouts or screams or ruddy oaths.

So, when he said, "Oh! Knocked him over! First cherry! Great yorker," you knew you'd just witnessed something special. Ever since YouTube came into being, I've gone back to that clip again and again. If there are two people to blame for me doing what I do now, it's Viv Richards for his 189 not out at Old Trafford in May 1984, and Benaud for that Morse-code-like description a few months later.

Most of all, though, when I think of Benaud, I feel pity, for the young fans of today and the noise pollution that they tend to be subjected to in the name of commentary. Of course, there are exceptions. The Sky team tends to treat the game with gravitas, and go beyond clichés, while the always perceptive Ian Chappell remains as a last link to Nine's golden years. Shane Warne, once removed from the blokey environs of the current Nine commentary enclosure, is well worth listening to, as is Rahul Dravid, whether on TV or radio.

Most, though, have nothing to offer. They long ago forgot the Benaud dictum of not saying anything just for the sake of it. Benaud was never a poet or a wordsmith in the John Arlott class. But he invariably had a pithy phrase for each notable occasion and, most importantly, he came prepared. You'd never have heard him express the kind of ignorance about a touring side that was on view during India's recent Test series in Australia.

That preparation came from an awareness of what the journalist's job entails. Unlike the buffoons of bluster, Benaud knew that the commentator and the columnist are just messengers, privileged to have a ringside view that others don't have access to. The game is never about them. They're just the thread that links the players on the field with millions of cricket-lovers around the world.

Benaud never made the commentary stint about him. He could have if he wanted to. After all, he had been one of the great all-rounders of his era. And as long as Test cricket is played, any discussion about its finest leaders will involve his name. But he wore that greatness as lightly as a cream linen suit. It was only years after first listening to him that some of us came to realise just how exceptional a player he had been.

That sadly is no longer the case. Those with CVs not even half as impressive swan about without even bothering to do basic research. They make no apology for being cheer-leaders. The "we", so anathema to Benaud – who had led his country with such distinction – is now the default setting. There's not even lip service to the idea of impartiality, and calling it as you see it.

But to remember Benaud only for his words is to do a great disservice to a man who was a pioneer in other ways as well. In an age when many Australian and English cricketers shied away from "hardship" tours of the subcontinent, Benaud saved some of his finest work for the most testing conditions, taking 71 wickets at 19.32 in 12 Tests across India and Pakistan. Gideon Haigh's magnificent *Summer Game* will tell you far more about the lasting legacy of some of those tours.

"A boy, just beginning, 25 years of age," began Benaud's tribute to Phillip Hughes last November. "Baggy Green No. 408. His father's best mate. Son. Brother. Fighter. Friend. Inspiration. Phillip Hughes. Forever. Rest in peace, son."

You could almost sense his voice breaking. Most of us would never hear from him again. Looking back, however, it was classic Benaud. Simple. Precise. Morse code. Using the least number of words to paint a picture beyond the scope of most ordinary mortals.

He truly was one of a kind.

Voice of Reason

*R*ichie Benaud's prowess elsewhere was so great that there is a danger of forgetting what a productive and gifted writer he was. There were numerous books, from Richie Benaud's Way of Cricket *in 1961 to* Over But Not Out *in 2010, and he was a columnist for the* News of the World *for 50 years. He first wrote for* Wisden *in 1962, paying tribute to his fellow Cricketer of the Year Alan Davidson. In the 1970s he became a regular at the front of the book, with essays on a variety of subjects, from fast bowlers ("the most exciting merchandise in cricket") to his favourite West Indians ("when he batted Worrell was rarely boorish enough to hit the ball"). First came an appreciation of the Ashes series of 1970-71 and 1972 – "the best cricket of any dual series since the war".*

SKILLS AND CONTROVERSY   Richie Benaud

It is rare for England and Australian spectators in the space of only 18 months to see two such splendidly assertive Test series as those played in 1970-71 and 1972. Six Tests in Australia and then five in England produced some top-class cricket and captaincy and, perhaps more important, provided a tremendous upsurge of interest in both countries. There were three captains involved in the series. First Bill Lawry and Ray Illingworth were in charge in 1970-71 but, towards the end of those Test matches, Lawry fell from grace and was replaced by Ian Chappell, who has led the Australian side ever since.

There is no more chancy game than cricket and it is worth pondering for a moment on what might have happened to the Australian captaincy had Dennis Lillee emerged as a fast bowler just one or two matches earlier than he eventually did. Lawry might have won a Test or two Tests and retained the captaincy, and Chappell could well still be Australia's vice-captain. Instead, it was Chappell who had the benefit of Lillee's emergence as a potentially great bowler and, in the series in England in 1972 and against Pakistan in 1972-73 in Australia, Chappell depended to a great extent on Lillee's ability.

For me, the last two series between England and Australia have been outstanding in their interest and in the skills shown by the players. There have been some who have decried the series in Australia when Illingworth regained the Ashes, and others who have found fault with most things which have happened in Anglo-Australian cricket for the past 18 months. I want to make it quite clear at the outset that I am not among those.

I thought the cricket was very good in Australia in 1970-71 and there was no doubt that England had the better side. I regarded Illingworth as a good skipper, despite what I reckon to be a palpable error in not making Australia follow on in the Adelaide Test of that series. This is not a case of being wise after the event, for I said exactly the same thing on the spot at the time. But, as always, it is a decision for the captain to make and, in the end, Illingworth could point to victory in the rubber and claim that he had been correct in allowing his bowlers that extra rest in Adelaide.

That series was, in fact, a good lead-up to the excitement of the 1972 battle in England, which produced some of the best cricket I have ever seen as a watcher. Indeed, to me, this was the best series I have had the pleasure of seeing since retiring as an active player. It brought on Ian Chappell as a captain, Lillee and Bob Massie as bowlers, Rod Marsh as an all-rounder and Greg Chappell and Ross Edwards as batsmen. For England it was a slightly different story and, as often happens with a team experienced both in years and cricketing knowhow, their cricket slipped a little.

When the Australians set out for their tour of the West Indies they had every cause to feel pleased with the way their cricket had staged a comeback, with the drawn series against England and their 3–0 victory over Pakistan to emphasise the improvement over the past 18 months.

Not the least interesting aspect of the past two Anglo-Australian series has been the amount of controversy engendered by the matches. Personally, I am all for a little bit of controversy in Test cricket, and I would require some convincing that events in the past two series have done the game the slightest bit of harm. On the contrary, I believe interest in cricket to have been stimulated rather than stilted by various events which have taken place on the field. In Australia it was the running battle between England's fast bowlers, and their skipper Illingworth, and the Australian umpire, Lou Rowan, and the spectators. In England it was the Headingley pitch, which raised a few eyebrows at a time when Australia had just squared the 1972 series.

Those who have never played Test cricket may find it hard to imagine exactly the atmosphere in the centre during a contest between two national teams. Cricketers who have never been in the press box or commented on Test matches would find it equally difficult to agree that controversy could be a good thing for cricket.

I believe the key to it lies in the modern-day attitude of the cricket spectator. In this I do not necessarily mean the man or woman who goes along to the ground having reserved a seat for a Test match day, sees that day's play and then goes home again and off to work for the remainder of the Test match. With television such a strong part of cricket these days, radio taking the game on to the beaches and into the homes and, as well, the spectators who go to the ground avidly watching every ball bowled, I feel there is a need for more than a stilted approach on the part of the players.

No spectator is particularly interested in seeing sportsmen perform on the field as would a group of stuffed dummies, neither is he interested in seeing what Australians would term a group of teddy bears in action on the ground or on the TV screen.

There have been a number of characters in cricket over the years and from old-time journalists we hear about them on many occasions. There was a time, not so long ago, when every effort was being made to stamp out the "character" of the players and have them conform to a rigid set of rules. Things have changed a little and both England and Australia can put into the field a number of players who are able to catch the spectator's eye whether batting, bowling, fielding, or just standing around as part of the team.

There will always be controversy where fast bowlers – and I mean fast bowlers, not the fast-medium, slogging-away variety – are involved in a cricket match. That extra pace, the judicious use of the bouncer as an attacking weapon and the ever-present chance of a batsman being hit – and painfully hit at that – all tend to keep in the fore-front of a spectator's mind that before him is a controversial character.

John Snow is one of these, off the field as quiet a man as you could wish to find and concentrating, they say, on his poetry to the exclusion of most other things. Be that as it may, on the field he is a dynamic proposition and a fine fast bowler. I was taken to task rather severely last year for having said on television that first of all I considered Snow to be a great bowler and secondly I could quite understand why he did not endeavour to bowl as fast and furiously for Sussex in seven-days-a-week cricket as he did in Test matches for England.

On that occasion I was pointing out the difference between English and Australian cricket where, in Australia, a bowler considers himself to have had a hard season if he has reached 250 overs by the conclusion of his eight matches. Whilst playing those games he will be giving himself "an easy" in club matches back in his own state. This aroused the indignation of a good many people who contended Snow should be bowling absolutely flat out for Sussex every time he picked up the ball. Sheer madness, I say.

Lillee would be finished in six months if he did this, and I have no doubt any England bowler would have the same happen to him if he were to carry out the strictures.

This is another reason why Snow himself is a controversial character, and it would be idle chatter to class him as the best-loved of the England Test team at the moment, certainly as far as administrators are concerned. He would be one of the best-loved in my team if he continued to bowl as he has done in the past two series between England and Australia. Even so, I doubt if he will ever be free from controversy, nor probably will Lillee, for the reasons expounded above.

There was no excuse, for example, for language allegedly used on the field to umpires in the 1970-71 series in

Australia, nor was there the slightest excuse for Illingworth wagging his finger in umpire Rowan's face during the final Test. That was merely provocative and, even worse, it was completely pointless.

At the same time, I was quite in accord with Illingworth when he took his players from the field whilst bottles and cans were removed from the playing area. I do not know that I would have flounced off the field with such determined indignation as Ray that day but I was certain at the time, and am still sure, he did the right thing in letting things settle down on the field and bringing his players back on once the ground had been cleared. Indeed, he had every right to insist, not ask, that the ground be cleared before play would continue.

Life was relatively placid from that incident through the Old Trafford Test at the start of the 1972 series, and through Lord's and Trent Bridge. The only ripples on the surface were the injury to Lillee's back, the splendid England win at Old Trafford and the astonishing bowling feat of Massie, playing in his first Test match at Lord's.

When I looked at the pitch set out for the Headingley Test in 1972, I must confess to having had a quiet chuckle to myself. If ever a game was labelled for controversy it was this one, to be played on a strip of earth so bare that one's neighbours would have laughed had it been put in the local lawn competition.

With Derek Underwood on hand, recalled to the England side, it became a good story for the press, radio and television and the two most important things were to have a copy of *Roget's Thesaurus* close at hand and to be able to judge when to book out of one's hotel, in the light of the game obviously not going the scheduled five days. In a situation such as that, a Test match can become just as much a battle between the media camps as between the players.

"Squealing Australians" was one popular phrase that was counteracted by apologies from other sections of those watching the game.

In the end, it did no harm at all far as I was concerned, because Australia squared the series at The Oval, and the image of the Test rubber as being very good for both spectators and players was retained right to the end.

Everyone will have their own ideas on this question of whether or not controversy harms cricket but, over the past two series between Australia and England, I think the game has come out of it very well. The type of controversy which I believe harms the game is where the cricketers are providing poor fare for the spectators, whether that be at the ground or on the television screens. This can come about in a variety of ways but more often in the past 20 years it has been because of unpardonably slow cricket.

There were days in these two series where the cricket was slow but it was thoroughly interesting and, at times, completely absorbing. At the end of a day's play the cricket watcher would have been so completely wrapped up in the events of the day that he would more than likely find it difficult to tell you off the cuff just how many runs had been scored per over.

Not so when there is any sort of deliberate attempt on the part of the fielding side to slow things down. I have absolutely no time for those who set out to contain a batting side by slowness in the field, dragging their feet in the change-over or in accentuating the slow walk back of the faster bowlers.

That sort of controversy I feel does harm in the game because it will be written up or talked about by the media and agreed with – as it should be – by the cricket follower. At this time cricket comes into disrepute and spectators have to decide whether or not they will go and watch a match in the light of the almost deliberate slowness of the players.

Personally, I think the last two series between these two countries have provided the best cricket of any dual series since the war. I thoroughly enjoyed the batting efforts of Geoffrey Boycott and John Edrich in Australia, the all-round ability of Basil D'Oliveira and the superb wicketkeeping of Alan Knott. Snow did a magnificent job for his captain and so did Peter Lever, Bob Willis and Underwood, who acted as perfect foils to Snow at the opposite end.

Although beaten, I enjoyed watching Keith Stackpole, Ian Redpath and the Chappell brothers, as well as Marsh, and, when these players and others went to England as a rough, untried team, there was plenty to appreciate in their play on the different style English pitches.

I doubt if cricket has ever had such beneficial publicity through all avenues of the media and rarely has the financial return been better for the game's administrators. I believe a great deal of this is due to the fact that in both series the cricket has been very good and the teams roughly equal in strength and intent on providing good entertainment. In addition, they have provided their share of controversy – or had it provided for them – and I regard that as a contributing factor to the success of the last 11 Test matches between England and Australia.

Gods or flannelled fools? Voiceless robots or men of character, willing and able to express their feelings? Well, you can take your pick, but I am inclined, having been both in the centre and in the press and television boxes, to prefer the latter any day.

From Wisden 1973

CRICKET FEVER HITS AUSTRALIA   Richie Benaud

England's cricket selectors, led by Alec Bedser, have the advantage over Australia in their bid to retain the Ashes in the series beginning in December, in that it is already clear that the Australian team will be chosen from an extremely small group of players. That is not to say it will not be a strong team, for no side boasting players of the calibre of the Chappell brothers, a refreshed Dennis Lillee, Doug Walters (on Australian pitches), Rod Marsh and Ashley Mallett is to be taken lightly. But when Bedser and his co-selectors sit down to choose their touring side, they will have before them the results of the 1973-74 Australian season as well as the short tour of New Zealand, and it will not be difficult to visualise the short list of players from whom the Australian First Test team would be chosen.

I make that point because it is a facet of selection not always recognised – the ability to evaluate the strength and personnel of the opposition, as well as the probable balance of their team. When the England touring team arrives in Australia it will be at a time when half of the last Australian team to tour England has been consigned to the pension department. Still on the Test scene will be Ian and Greg Chappell, Mallett, Walters, Marsh, plus the new hope of the selectors, 21-year-old Ian Davis. Also available will be Keith Stackpole, Paul Sheahan, Ian Redpath, Lillee, Ross Edwards and Graeme Watson, but I doubt there will be much sign of Bruce Francis, John Inverarity, Brian Taber, Jeff Hammond, David Colley, John Gleeson and Bob Massie. The Australian selectors have had their problems over the past 12 months, and they have compounded them by playing their hunches more often than most selection committees will do in a lifetime.

Davis is an interesting young player. Brought into the New South Wales team as a surprise selection after the start of the 1972-73 season, he took his chance well and showed more promise than anyone to come from that state for some years. He is slim and quick moving, an elegant stroke-player who elicited from the old-timers sobriquets of "another Jackson", "another Kippax", etc. If he merely continues to be a Davis it should be enough for the present. It is most unusual for a player to be given an Australian cap after only five Sheffield Shield matches and, personally, I would have preferred to see him go through a slightly tougher grooming that would have better fitted him for a series against England with the Ashes at stake. Australians will be hoping that his excellent temperament will take the strain when the matches that matter get under way. If Frank Hayes goes to Australia, there could be quite a battle between the fair-haired pair for the title of best young batsman of the series.

With this season of matches against India and Pakistan to guide them, the England selectors should be able to nominate a strong touring side and hopefully, by its play, one that will be able to continue the resurgence of Australian cricket interest so evident in the past two years. Australian cricket seems to go in cycles. There was the great era of Don Bradman's team just after the war, then the slump as most of those players came to the end of their careers. Frank Worrell's West Indian side did wonders for our cricket from 1960 to 1963, but the retirement of key players meant another rebuilding period, with consequent loss of spectator appeal, and now Chappell's team, starting in 1972, is touching the same high point. How long it can last is the crucial question – but certainly, for the moment, cricket in Australia has an interest rating as high as I have ever known it.

England's players and followers who recall the Brisbane Gabba ground as one of the least attractive aspects of an Australian tour, and who remember the lack of spectator support in Brisbane, will get a real shock in December. Cricket fever has hit the town with the move of Greg Chappell from South Australia, and their wonderful performances in the Sheffield Shield and Gillette Cup have made cricket the number one sport in the north. In addition, the ground is a picture; a credit to the authorities who have put up new grandstands, planted shrubs and trees, relaid the pitch and produced an outfield rated now as the best in Australia. Players like Denis Compton, able to recall the ramshackle amenities of their day, will find it hard to believe.

There was a general increase in crowds attending cricket matches in the past two seasons in Australia, though overall attendances in Tests have fallen in the past ten years. Board of Control members responsible for the sharing out of profits will be hoping that the England–Australia clashes this time will draw more rather than fewer spectators, though they are well aware that there is far greater interest in the game now in Australia than at any other time in those ten years.

It is the same situation in England, where spectators find it hard to get time off work to watch cricket and are happy to use their transistor radios and watch television as an alternative to going to the grounds. Ratings of the Australian Broadcasting Commission cricket telecast have zoomed and, when the six Tests are played in Australia on the coming tour, over three million calls will be made to the Post Office sports results service... that figure will drop to half a million for a month as soon as the Tests are finished.

Such has been the interest in the game over the past season in Australia that the Gillette Cup matches have been televised by commercial stations as well as the ABC – a real breakthrough in taking the game into hundreds of thousands of homes. For one such one-day match in Australia there were three TV stations in action at the Adelaide Oval, a sight calculated to ease the ulcers of sponsors and cricket administrators alike.

The 1974 English season also has much to live up to, for the cricket played in 1973 in England was almost uniformly good and compared favourably with the 1972 season. The exception, of course, was that miserable match at Edgbaston, where rain would have been a merciful saviour. I suppose in the midst of all the good cricket from England, New Zealand and the West Indies, it had to happen that one match was a disaster, but shortly after it was made up for, in part, by the splendid performance at Lord's.

For the moment anyway, it seems that the problem has been solved of spectators running on to the field when the game is in progress, though I hope English administrators will be firm in their approach to this question when their team comes to Australia. For some years in Australia ground authorities have allowed children and adults to rush the field when fifties and centuries were scored by batsmen, but it got so out of hand that all states apart from New South Wales have clamped down on the practice. The season just complete has produced two instances of players being jostled rather than congratulated, and the final blow was when one teenage lout poured a can of beer over the century-maker, Ian Davis, at the Sydney Cricket Ground. As that ground was the scene of the can-throwing and England team walkoff in the final Test of 1970-71, I should have thought the Cricket Association concerned would have been keen to protect the players from this type of pseudo hero-worship. Unless administrators from both countries are firm in their attitude on this question, I believe we will have a nasty incident, quite apart from the irritating delays in play to which other spectators are subject. It is a matter that should be high on the list of the England manager when he is chosen.

Tours of England by India and Pakistan appear to come thick and fast these days and, with some splendid cricketers in both visiting sides, England cricket followers should be in for a real treat as a prelude to the touring team for Australia being chosen. As India has twice beaten England in the most recent series between the two countries, there is reason to hope for a magnificent summer of quality cricket.

1973 was a fascinating season, with New Zealand almost recording their first victory against England, West Indies climbing back off the floor after the disappointments of the series against Australia a few months earlier, and the haggling over the England captaincy where Ray Illingworth eventually had to make way for Mike Denness.

In many ways, this was the end of an era for English cricket, for Illingworth had regained the Ashes during his reign and, as well, had captained England purposefully over the period from June 1969, when he was successful in his first match as captain against the West Indies. I always had a most healthy respect for him as a leader; a shrewd, practical captain and a man who was at his best when things were not going well for his side. The captain of the England team against India and Pakistan and Australia has much to live up to over the next 12 months.

One unknown quantity as far as the Australian and England selection committees are concerned will be Lillee, who bowled in such fiery fashion against England in 1972. The three stress fractures of his back have completely healed, but he contented himself with bowling in club rather than first-class matches in the last Australian season, stating that he wanted to be completely fit to greet the England batsmen when they arrived in Australia. If fully fit, he will add thousands to the gate, interest to the series and pleasure to Ian Chappell's continued stint as Australian captain. Such is the rating given him by every cricket follower in Australia as they follow the series of matches between England, India and Pakistan and prepare for the battle for the Ashes over the ensuing few months.

From Wisden 1974

ELEVEN WEST INDIES MEN OF MY TIME   Richie Benaud

If one word had to be used to describe West Indian cricket at Test level it would be "unpredictable". Exciting yes, enthusiastic certainly, friendly by all means, and often electric, but *unpredictable* stands out from all the others. They can turn a Test match their way in a couple of astonishing overs, sometimes they can turn it the opposition's way with a burst of excess zeal that loses wickets, drops catches, provides run-outs and generally drives their supporters to distraction.

It is not easy to come up with the best 11 players spanning a period of a quarter of a century, but it brings the memories flooding back. I first played against them in 1951-52 when John Goddard's team came to Australia and had lost the series 3–1 by the time the Fifth Test was played. The Australian selectors chose to blood three young players for the final Test – Colin McDonald, George Thoms and me – and there was no shortage of excitement over the next four days, with Keith Miller and Ray Lindwall bowling on a green Sydney pitch and letting the West Indian batsmen have their fair share of bumpers. Some said more than their fair share but, at the time and now, I could see nothing outside the rules in the manner in which either man bowled.

Everton Weekes, Frank Worrell and Clyde Walcott were in that team, and Walcott in particular extracted some revenge three years later when we went to the West Indies by hitting a string of centuries against us. It was quite an experience playing in the West Indies that year and, on those pitches and against those batsmen, one's bowling experience was enriched; not all of it pleasantly.

Although it was 20 years ago, I vividly remember just one over I bowled to Walcott in the opening Test of that series at Sabina Park, Jamaica. The ground is small, the pitch is like a piece of reddish-coloured glass, the outfield is like lightning. At the end of the innings the bowling analysis read Benaud 19–7–29–0, and it is one of those maidens to which I refer. In the covers was Neil Harvey, at extra cover Ron Archer, at mid-off Arthur Morris. At the end of the over they were covered in dust from diving either to the right or left, skidding along the turf to cut off six magnificent drives off back and front foot by Walcott. There should have been 24 runs from the over – if ever there was a deceitful statistic it was the one in that maidens column.

Walcott was a dynamic player, a man of immense strength who hit the ball like a thrashing machine with a great whirling of the bat. There was nothing at all elegant about him… or was there? Could anyone be brutally elegant? If the answer is yes, that was Walcott – the perfect complement to the other Ws. He was a more than useful wicketkeeper and could bowl medium-pace as well, as he proved when back trouble cut short his keeping career, but it was in the tremendous power of his strokeplay that I best remember him.

Weekes was one of the greatest batsmen I ever watched, even though I only saw him when that wasted leg muscle was restricting his footwork. He had one of the widest bats I have ever seen from 22 yards, and that Yorkshire adage of "show 'em the maker's name" might have been devised just for him. Memory tells me that he had the back of his left hand facing a little more to the bowler than normal – perhaps that had something to do with the straightness of his play – but unfortunately for the bowler he was also wonderfully and successfully unorthodox when he wished. He made 139 and 87 not out against us in Trinidad in 1955 and 81 at Georgetown but he was never quite himself in that series, nor against England in 1957.

Frank Maglinne Worrell… now there was elegance for you. There was a man for all summers. I did not believe it when Miller told me Frank used to prepare for battle by having a sleep with the pads on on the massage table. True. A wonderfully relaxed person, and one of the great men ever to grace any sporting field. I ran him out in my first Test in Sydney with a throw from midwicket, but nine years later he was back again, captaining West Indies with such calm authority and wonderful flair that spectators watched one of the greatest Test series of all time. For Worrell to captain West Indies required quite a change in thinking on the part of the West Indies Board of Control; for him to make a success of it was therefore doubly important. For his many friends and advocates in the West Indies it was vital.

I remember meeting him at Sydney Airport when the West Indies team arrived in 1960 and, in the course of chatting, he said he thought we would have a lot of fun during the summer. At the time he was not having much fun as he was suffering with shellfish poisoning picked up on the way to Australia. Not only did we have a lot of fun but so too did the spectators, with the freak results obtained in the summer.

There was no more elegant mover in the game in my time – Australians tell me Alan Kippax and Archie Jackson were his equivalent, though I can hardly believe it. He moved with the sleepy grace generally associated with the cat family, and when he batted he was rarely boorish enough to hit the ball.

Occasionally he stroked it but mostly he caressed it through the covers or past mid-on, sometimes there was a flick past square leg as a concession to conventional power. A great player, a great man and a wonderful servant to cricket.

Of course that trio must go into any West Indies team in the past 25 years, and this then restricts the batting places available in any combination. Garry Sobers is the all-rounder at seven, Rohan Kanhai must play at No. 3 as one of the finest batsmen the world has seen. That leaves the openers to complete the batting line-up and here I would use Conrad Hunte and Seymour Nurse, the former a splendid player of the new ball and of all types of spin bowling, and Nurse a most underrated player in my opinion. I went on tour with him some years ago and not many batsmen could have played better.

With Kanhai at No. 3 and Sobers at No. 7 flanking the Three Ws, it is a terrifying batting line-up. When Kanhai and Sobers came to Australia in 1960-61 there was intense competition between them as to which one would score most runs. This is the sort of competition an opposing bowler like myself or Alan Davidson could do without, for both of them took dismissal as a personal affront. On that tour I thought Kanhai just shaded Sobers with the bat, but then the latter had his four styles of bowling to lift him to the class of a great all-rounder. Both were fine fieldsmen and wonderful close-to-the-wicket catchers.

With Walcott keeping wicket, that leaves four bowlers to be included. and I go for two from my era around the 1960s and two from the early 1950s – Wes Hall and Lance Gibbs, Sonny Ramadhin and Alf Valentine. Although I actually played against all four, it was in those periods named that they were at their peak.

"Ram and Val" had their own calypso... an anthem would not have been out of place for the deeds they managed when West Indian cricket was pummelling England in 1950. Ramadhin, the little mystery spinner who turned the ball both ways on English pitches but was more restricted in Australia, burst on to the cricket scene in that summer when hardly any English batsmen could consistently lay the bat on him. At the other end, Valentine was spinning his fingers raw with his delightfully orthodox action – the perfect complement to his partner. By the time they came to Australia, in 1960, they were past their best, and when Harvey gave "Ram" some stick in the Melbourne Test of that series the West Indies tour selectors dropped him in favour of a spindly youngster named Gibbs who looked as though a substantial meal would do him more good than 20 overs in a Test match.

He soon showed us all about that! Magnificent bowling in the next Test in Sydney was followed by the hat-trick in Adelaide (as I watched from the non-striker's end) and some more superb bowling in the final match in Melbourne. Not even greying hair will stop him from beating Freddie Trueman's record haul of wickets in Test cricket to give West Indies the dual honour of most runs (Sobers) and most wickets (Gibbs) in the history of the game.

At the other end, in most of Gibbs' triumphs over the following eight years, was Wesley Winfield Hall, now Senator

Hall, who was one of the great fast bowlers the cricket world has seen. Miller and Lindwall, Lillee and Thomson, Tyson and Statham, Gregory and McDonald?… Hall was on his own when I played against him in 1960, as indeed was Davidson in the time he took the new ball for Australia from 1958 to 1963.

Worrell and Sobers shared the new ball with him at different times but the "big fella" did it the hard way until Charlie Griffith came along.

How would you like to face that line-up on the first morning of the opening Test match at Lord's or the Sydney Cricket Ground?

1. C. C. Hunte, 2. S. M. Nurse, 3. R. B. Kanhai, 4. E. D. Weekes, 5. C. L. Walcott (wicketkeeper), 6. F. M. M. Worrell (captain), 7. G. S. Sobers (vice-captain), 8. W. W. Hall, 9. L. R. Gibbs, 10. S. Ramadhin, 11. A. L. Valentine.

I do not think the opposing batsmen would be all that happy in any conditions, opposing bowlers would simply be tired!

From Wisden 1976

FROM SPOFFORTH TO LILLEE   Richie Benaud

Right from the time Fred Spofforth bowled out England in that famous Test at The Oval and Ernest Jones slipped his faster one through W. G.'s beard at Sheffield Park, Sussex, fast bowlers have been the most exciting merchandise in cricket. Oh, I know they called Bradman "The Don" and Everton Weekes the "Barbados Butcher", but even those nicknames scarcely convey the menace of "Demon" Spofforth or "Typhoon" Tyson in full cry. In the two Tests of the 1954-55 series in Sydney and Melbourne, the

"Typhoon" was the fastest bowler I ever faced. The Sydney pitch was so green it could hardly be distinguished from the rest of the square and the Melbourne one so dry that it was thought necessary to give it a subtle hosing on the rest day, lest the saucer-shaped depressions point themselves skywards the next day.

Fast bowlers capture public imagination. At the same time they make the hearts of opposing batsmen beat a little faster and there is no question in my mind that they draw spectators through the turnstiles with their searing pace, gesticulations and all-out attack. Real fast bowlers I am talking about. The ones no one likes to bat against. I know there have been some old-timers who have gone on record saying "the faster they bowl the harder I'll hit 'em". Those are not bowlers of the pace of Larwood or Voce we are talking about, or before them Gregory or McDonald. Don't be misled into thinking that anyone ever fancied themselves against Miller or Lindwall, Tyson, Trueman, Statham, Snow or Lillee and Thomson, even if the pitch were perfect for batting. Provide a surface with a little variable bounce and it was absolute hell for the batsmen. I suppose cricketers who are expert batsmen, bowlers (slow) and fieldsmen may cavil at the thought of fast bowlers being more exciting, but in my own section of leg-spinning there was only ever one bowler considered volatile enough to warrant the name "Tiger".

The rest of us were simply rated as "thoughtful" with the occasional exception of "cunning". So be it. After all we scarcely put as much exciting physical effort into the game as do our faster counterparts. Rarely do you hear of a slow bowler who has gone in the back as Dennis Lillee did in the West Indies in 1973, though there have been a few slow bowlers like myself who have had shoulder trouble from flexing of the wrist.

The question of the pace of fast bowlers of different generations is as vexing as posing the question of who has been the greatest batsman in the world. Or was as vexing. With the electronic and computer methods available these days, experts can calculate that Lillee bowls at around 95mph, Jeff Thomson a fraction faster, and that they average something like 85mph.

Were Jack Gregory and Ted McDonald faster than that? Did they even remotely approach those figures? Well, the editor of *Wisden*, having seen them bowl at Lionel Tennyson in the 1921 series in England, gave them a rating of 60mph. It is possible he was correct, but from what I have heard they were just as quick as a lot of the faster bowlers of modern days. I hope so, or a lot of the dreams of the older players will have faded away.

Speed is relative. It is relative to the batsman you are bowling against, to the pitch condition, to the atmosphere, but in the end, if you are talking about brute speed there is not much in it when you compare a number of really fast men.

I'm certain, for example, that Frank Tyson when measured on a modern-day electronic framing machine would bowl as fast as Thomson most of the time... faster at times. Thomson's new style action poses problems and might give him an extra yard in pace before the batsman is able to focus on the ball.

Tyson and Brian Statham were the first really fast bowlers I batted against in first-class cricket.

When I came on to the first-class scene Keith Miller and Ray Lindwall also played for New South Wales and although there were some other pace bowlers around at that time these two were easily the fastest. Lindwall is the best fast bowler I have ever seen from the technical point of view, even though the purists may say that his arm was a fraction too low in delivery. There are others of whom the purists say that their arm has been too high, so there is no guarantee that the player himself is wrong. Lindwall, in fact, could hardly have been more successful with a method that allowed him to have his outswinger snapping away from right-handers and coming back late at left-handers. He didn't bother about an inswinger until, playing in the Lancashire League for a season, he discovered that the best way of making certain of taking wickets, and therefore a collection, was to bowl out the batsmen rather than rely on the slip catches to be taken.

Because he was as shrewd a campaigner as I have seen, he allied that inswinger to his leg-cutter and a batsman after that time could never really be certain if the ball would swing in, or, having been held across the seam, would cut away. Once in a match in Sydney when New South Wales played Victoria, I persuaded him to bowl it first ball of the second innings to the Test opener Colin McDonald. Colin knew that "Lindy" liked to warm up with an over or so before loosing the inswinger at the batsman. It was the most perfectly pitched delivery. Colin shuffled across to allow the outswinger to pass and the flurried defensive stroke missed the ball by six inches and I have scarcely ever seen a more adjacent lbw turned down. I had the feeling that the umpire was as surprised as the batsman, as he too had never seen Lindwall bowl an inswinger first ball of an innings.

They were a great combination, Lindwall and Miller, both all-rounders, in fact, I felt that Lindwall was always underrated in that department. He was a fine hard-hitting batsman with a flourish in the backswing, and although he went in late for Australia he still played many innings of distinction.

Miller was in the great class as an all-rounder. A flamboyant cricketer and a great character, he was the best all-round cricketer I ever played with or against. Garry Sobers later made his name in the same area and is classed by many now as the greatest cricketer ever to play the game because of the many things he could do so well. But in that 1948–1963 period I never saw another cricketer to equal Miller.

He was a dynamic batsman, a brilliant fieldsman and his batting could have earned him a place in any Australian Test era. But it was as Lindwall's partner that he was most famous, and he was the perfect man to have at the other end. Whereas Lindwall was slightly round-arm and was skidding at you, Miller was all upright delivery, hair awry, and was lifting the ball from even the most sluggish surface at around your ribs. It was as they were coming to the end of their time that Tyson and Statham came on the scene.

I played in the Australian XI game against MCC in Melbourne in 1954, and Statham was on his own then. He posed enough problems for me and for the other Australian batsmen on trial, and I had a fair guide to his pace because I had hit a century off Lindwall in Brisbane a couple of weeks earlier. He bowled very well to take four wickets on an unresponsive surface, but it was a rude shock to find that Statham was making me hurry my shot a little. It was an even ruder shock the following week to bat at No. 3 against Tyson at the Sydney Cricket Ground and find him sliding at me from 20 yards at the Randwick End and having to fend one away from my chin to first slip.

I had seen him before. In the 1953 tour of England, Northamptonshire produced him against us and he bowled Graeme Hole and hit McDonald on the foot so hard that had he not been lbw he could not have continued his innings for a considerable time. Neil Harvey then proceeded to hit a century before lunch, but Tyson's speed had not been forgotten. When he came to Australia he had a run up so long that in the first match at Bunbury, in much the same manner as Wes Hall in Jamaica, he would begin his run by pushing off the sightscreen. Unfortunately for Australia, common sense prevailed in the end and he was persuaded to shorten his run and he was immediately a better and faster bowler.

Frank was never quite the same again after that tour, but it was no real pleasure to bat against him and Statham in those Tests, on at least two pitches that were difficult. The best fast-bowling combinations are the ones with one fine supporting bowler. Miller and Lindwall had Bill Johnston, as good a fast-medium left-hander as you could ever hope to bat against. "Large" took the new ball for Victoria and bowled more bumpers at the opposing batsmen than any other bowler around at that time. The difference was that he never snarled at you. He always offered that wonderful throaty chuckle and there is no batsman born who could possibly take offence at that.

Umpires, keen to see their frames on the television screens these days, could have had a field day with him, but, I suspect, even in these modern times they would have been as friendly to him as the batsmen. If he was the perfect foil to Miller and Lindwall, so was Trevor Bailey to Tyson and Statham… Trevor was not necessarily everyone's idea of an entertaining batsman, but as third seamer to that pair he was just about ideal. Mostly outswing, sometimes the one coming back the other way and a good deal of movement off the pitch.

They are the lucky ones, the fast bowlers with the third seamer to assist them. But what about the ones who did it all on their own… in single file. Although this is an article to do with fast bowlers it would be sacrilege to omit mention of Alec Bedser, Alan Davidson and Graham McKenzie, all of whom had the misfortune to play their best cricket for

England and Australia in an era when there was no other experienced fast bowler at the opposite end. Bedser was one of the real greats for England. I had first-hand knowledge of Davidson as I captained him from 1958 onwards, and then McKenzie carried the Australian attack from 1964 to 1969. What they would have been like if there had been an express bowler at the other end and the batsmen were trying to get down to *their* end is a mind-boggling exercise.

Freddie Trueman bowled splendidly for England as a raw youngster in 1952, then did army service and played against us in 1953 in the final Test before going to the West Indies in 1953-54 and missing the tour to Australia in 1954-55. He bowled superbly in 1958-59 and 1961, but he was more a craftsman than an express bowler.

Generally when captains set out to win a series for England or Australia they have bowling trumps at their disposal. When Ray Illingworth planned his campaign in 1970 he had John Snow and some courageous but lesser lights at his disposal. Snow in the 1970-71 series was a great bowler in Australia, fast and aggressive, able to move the ball in the air and off the seam and, despite anything the batsman did, able to keep an almost perfect line and length.

In the Fifth Test of that series in Adelaide I had my first sight of Lillee. Long black hair, thinnish build and a sprawling delivery stride couldn't disguise the fact that here Australia had something for the future. He bowled with great enthusiasm and, for the amount of experience he had to that date, with a great deal of skill and temperament, and England's batsmen were in no doubt that they had seen a star of the future. Since then he has become a wonderful bowler; a fluent action, ability to change his pace and move the ball either way off the seam or in the air, and a tremendous temperament have made him one of the real greats as far as I am concerned. Anyone who can fight back as he did with that back injury of three stress fractures is tops for courage. He was lucky that in 1973 the Australian selectors took a chance with some fellow with a funny action named Thomson. He looked a little like a javelin thrower, with the crossed feet in delivery stride and the hiding of the ball from the batsman by propelling it from behind the right thigh instead of the shoulder. Just think, some coach might have got hold of Thommo a few years ago and said to him, "Look here son... you'll never get anywhere this way... try it the orthodox way."

Together Lillee and Thomson are the fastest *pair* I have ever seen.

You can throw in Hall and Griffith, Tyson and Statham, Miller and Lindwall, and if I had to choose one pair it would be Lillee and Thomson. What... just what... would they have done if they had played in the late 1940s when administrators gave fast bowlers the chance of having a new ball every 40 overs in Australia and every 55 overs in England?

From Wisden 1977

EFFECTS OF THE BUMPER – HAS IT RUINED BATSMANSHIP?
Richie Benaud

The popular theory these days is that the bumper has ruined Australian batsmanship. Ruined is too harsh a word for me. "Changed" I could come to terms with, but, even then, it is an over-simplification. A bumper changes nothing really, nor does it affect anything unless it is a good bumper posing problems to the batsman. And the batsman, correspondingly, must be a poor hooker, or at least play a poor stroke, for it to have the slightest effect on him.

At least as popular as the above theory is the one that states that more bumpers are bowled these days. Memories are short. When I first came into the game just on 30 years ago as a player, Ray Lindwall and Keith Miller were letting fly, then Frank Tyson, Brian Statham, Fred Trueman, Neil Adcock, Peter Heine, Wes Hall and Charlie Griffith, followed by John Snow, moved on to the turn of the 1960s. I refuse to believe more bumpers are bowled these days than by that group. I was either on the receiving end of a lot of them or was watching from slip or the pavilion.

A few months ago in Sydney I met Adcock again, and we swapped stories as middle-aged ex-sportsmen tend to do. Naturally, we both bowled and batted a little better than 20 years earlier but, on one thing, we were agreed – that, comparatively, it is highly unlikely that any more bumpers would ever be bowled than in that 1957-58 series in South Africa.

There are very few good players of really fast bowling. The stories of olden-day batsmen relishing fast bowling, even on untrue pitches, are, to me, a piece of whimsy. I have great difficulty in believing that anyone could look forward to facing Tyson, Lindwall, Miller, Jeff Thomson and Dennis Lillee on a fast, bouncy pitch such as Perth. You take your chance and you do not worry about being hit. As soon as you begin to worry about that aspect of batting you should be back in club cricket playing for Saturday afternoon pleasure.

To achieve a balance on whether or not the bumper has had an effect on Australian batsmanship, it is necessary to trace the history of Australian batsmen and opposing express bowlers over the years. "Express" is the operative word. An ordinary fast-medium bowler who lets go a bouncer is just asking for trouble, unless it is played with a quick, quick, slow foxtrot towards the square-leg umpire. Max Walker, for example, should never be guilty of letting go a bumper – every time he does, it should be money for old rope.

The day I was born in 1930, the Australian team were returning by boat from England where Don Bradman and Bill Ponsford had thrashed the opposing bowlers. The story goes that Bodyline was born on the final afternoon when Bradman and Archie Jackson had to bat on a wet pitch. I find that difficult to believe. No captain would produce such a controversial scheme on the evidence of one short spell when the next tour was to be played on the bone-hard pitches of Australia.

Bumpers and the Bodyline field settings certainly ruined Australian batsmanship for a time. I am not surprised. I have often wondered how I would have played Bodyline. Having talked with Bradman, Jack Fingleton, the late Stan McCabe and Bill O'Reilly about it, the answer is that I just could not have managed it. I was a compulsive hooker and I guess I would have changed to being a compulsive ducker and weaver.

At 16, I first saw Lindwall and Miller in action and, because of their dominance in the fast-bowling world, bumpers were not a dirty word to Australian batsmen until 1954. Really then, there was a time span of 20 years (including war time) when Australian batsmen had little experience of short-pitched express bowling, other than in Sheffield Shield cricket. And I can assure you I was quite delighted when both Miller and Lindwall finished playing for New South Wales where I lived. Other Australians had other ideas. When New South Wales played Queensland on a greentop one year, players like Ken Archer and Colin McCool, both splendid cricketers, found themselves playing most of the time between waist and throat level. My arrival at the crease with the ball was usually greeted, if not with a war cry, at least with barely disguised pleasure, bordering on contempt.

Batsmen like Arthur Morris, Sidney Barnes, Neil Harvey and Sam Loxton of the 1948 tour of England were all virile players of the hook and pull, so too Bradman; but that changed for an Australian batsman when Tyson, Statham and Trueman came along, with Peter Loader as very useful back-up material. Almost immediately Adcock and Heine were into us, and Hall was there in 1960-61.

There was a definite change in Australian batting against bumpers over that period. Jim Burke had retired in 1959, Colin McDonald, Bob Simpson and Bill Lawry were the openers in the early 1960s and almost until 1970 – but it had been an unsettling time before that. Tyson and Statham produced a lot of playing across the line of the ball in 1954-55. So too did Hall in 1960-61. It is there I believe that the clue lies to Australians', and perhaps any other batsman's, skill against the bumper. Their batting can be ruined if the bumper causes them to change their style and play across the line.

Doug Walters is the classic example. It is the short-pitched delivery which dismisses Doug in, say, 80% of cases. Not directly, mind you, and I do not need a memory jog to tell me about Doug's record. I generally remind other people of it. But, being an admirer of his unorthodox skills and exceptional temperament should not blind one to the short-comings. If you study his technique with the naked eye and on slow-motion replays, it is easy to see that indeed on occasions the bumper has ruined his batsmanship. He ducks and bobs and squats, and when the short-of-a-length ball comes along around the off stump he is never quite in position to play it. The two gullies and three slips are on their toes ball by ball. That, I hasten to say, is not meant to be a full explanation, because Walters is just as likely to come out tomorrow and paste the fast bowlers all round the ground, as he did in Perth in 1974 on a fast, bouncy pitch. There he brought up his hundred with a marvellous pull for six off Bob Willis from the last ball of the day.

Where I think the bumper has definitely changed Australian batsmanship in recent times is at the top of the order. Let's go back for a moment to the mid-1960s, where we had McDonald, Simpson and Lawry at the start of a ten-year span. Colin did not hook. The fast bowlers quickly got to know this and had to change their technique. It was just as painful I suppose to Colin to be hit on the thigh or in the ribs, but not as dangerous as hooking or being hit on the head.

Simpson did not hook at all. He devised his own method of weaving away to the leg side and he played the short-pitched bowling well, even though at times it looked a little strange. Ian Redpath followed that technique and, although he always looked awkward, he rarely got out. Lawry hooked and hooked well, but he was very selective. Then Keith Stackpole was elevated from the middle of the order and he was a brilliant hooker and puller.

Since that time it is hard to think of anyone to match those players in skill against the short-pitched ball. Graeme Watson, who opened occasionally, Alan Turner, Rick McCosker and Ian Davis are all indifferent players of the bumper, and this indecisiveness affects their footwork in the playing of other strokes. Mostly in recent years Ian Chappell has been coming in to bat with the shine still on the ball, so too his brother Greg when he took over the No. 3 position. Both are hookers, and good ones, though at times Ian has found problems with the stroke, but in both these cases it could hardly be said that the bumper has ruined their batting. The answer probably is a cliché... class will out. The outstanding batsman is outstanding against any bowler and any ball.

However, sitting back now and having looked at the Australian side of things, it is worth looking at all the other countries as well. Has the bumper ruined Indian batsmanship? It certainly does when they see one. There are no bumpers in India from fast bowlers because there are no fast bowlers. The same applies to Pakistan, but their batsmen like Mushtaq Mohammad, Zaheer Abbas, Asif Iqbal and Sadiq Mohammad all play the short ball extremely well. Probably they see a few in English county cricket, but when they play the West Indians and the Australians they are given plenty of practice. The Indians do not have a sound track record, and against pace in Australia last summer they were inclined to shuffle a little.

And what of the West Indians? They are regarded as the finest players in the world of the short-pitched ball. To see Viv Richards batting against Lillee is to see the ultimate in battles between bat and the fast ball. Clive Lloyd is tremendously powerful pulling and hooking. Yet in 1975-76 in Australia, only one of their Tests against Australia went past four days and then only minimally. Thomson, Lillee and Gary Gilmour took 29, 27 and 20 wickets respectively, and the hook shot caused most of the chaos. My first sight of the West Indians was in 1951-52, when Miller and Lindwall were at top pace. The West Indians wilted against the short ball, but then so would anyone else have wilted against that pair.

Englishmen have the same problems. Take David Steele, for example. When the Australians were in England in 1975 he was a hero. The following summer against the West Indians he again performed creditably in the opening Tests, but later his keenness to get on to the front foot against all bowlers allowed the bumper to destroy him. He missed the tour of India and was not seen in a Test in 1977.

It is then, I believe, a matter of technique, as is the ability to combat the good outswinger or inswinger. The fine pace bowler who delivers two searing outswingers and then cuts the next one back off the seam has an outstanding chance of taking a wicket. Equally, the chance is there for the bumper used, say, in two ways… a couple of good bouncers in one over and then the outswinger well pitched up on the off stump to draw the batsman into the stroke. Or a couple of good outswingers followed by the bumper that slants in at the batsman and cramps him for room. Thomson bowls the latter ball very well – it seems to follow the batsman and gives him little chance of getting inside the line to pull and hook. Alan Davidson could do the same because of the angle, though I hasten to add, for Thommo's benefit, not at the same pace.

I suppose that this discussion is as inconclusive as most other cricket arguments between players and ex-players. But I definitely could come to terms with the thought that in the past seven years the bumper has had some effect on bats-manship in all countries, particularly Australia. Watching hours of slow-motion replays recently has bolstered my argument that runs along the line of the best players in any era being able to play any type of ball, but players of lesser quality change their method when really fast bowlers come on.

The change, simply put, is that they suddenly begin to play across the ball instead of through it, and I offer it not as a criticism but a fact from the replays. Having said that, I am immediately reminded that, playing golf last summer in a Pro-Am with Ken Barrington, he offered the same opinion. I had the "yips" at the time with my putting and did not pay him full attention, but he was absolutely right. Perhaps the Australian players, and those from other countries so afflicted, should spend a few hours in the videotape studios instead of in the nets!

From Wisden 1977

In the late 1970s, Kerry Packer's revolution changed cricket forever. Benaud reflected on the impact of World Series Cricket in his foreword for the Wisden Anthology 1978–2006.

Wisden tells us everything about the game of cricket, always has from the time of the first issue. From the moment I read my first copy during the Australian tour of 1953, I've always thought that a story lies in every one of the hundreds of pages. One of the very biggest, part of cricket's evolution, came in the 1978 edition. This covered the 1977 formation of World Series Cricket, and the ensuing meetings of the International Cricket Conference and the High Court hearing. After 31 days, Mr Justice Slade found on all counts for World Series Cricket and for the three players, Tony Greig, John Snow and Mike Procter. He ruled that the ICC resolutions had been in "unreasonable restraint of trade". In a delicious touch of irony, the 1978 *Wisden* story began opposite an item on page 122 recalling that coloured shirts, which had been commonly worn, had disappeared from cricket in the period 1880–1895.

World Series Cricket began in 1977, but the seeds that would produce cricket's age of revolution had been sown earlier. In 1976, Channel Nine had offered the Australian Board of Control $1,500,000 for three years' television coverage of Australian cricket; the board, though, accepted a $200,000 offer for three years from the Australian Broadcasting Commission – quite a difference by way of income for grassroots cricket. No one, other than the people concerned on the board and those from Channel Nine, had any inkling this had happened.

By chance, however, this coincided with meetings of aggrieved and extremely disgruntled Australian cricketers who had been trying for four years, without the slightest success, to improve their payments from the board. One of the players' meetings had been with Bob Hawke, a cricket-lover and astute politician who had advised the players that under no circumstances in their discussions with the board should they indicate they were thinking along the lines of forming a union. It should only be noted as a Players' Association.

One of the more significant happenings had occurred in 1975, when Ian Chappell was captain of the Australian team that travelled to England via Canada for the inaugural World Cup. Chappell, who was both international cricketer and professional journalist, had advised the Australian Cricket Board he would be writing articles for newspapers whilst on tour. He received a letter informing him that this was not possible and he was not, under any circumstances, to have cricket articles published during the tour. Both Chappell and I were members of the Australian Journalists' Association which in May 1975 wrote to Sir Donald Bradman expressing concern that Chappell and Ashley Mallett, also a professional journalist, appeared to be bound by restrictive Cricket Board legislation that affected their livelihoods.

Sir Donald was sufficiently concerned to make enquiries in several areas. As a result, he was left in no doubt, if the Australian cricket authorities challenged either the Journalists' Association or the players, Chappell and Mallett, the board would certainly lose the case because they were *restraining the trade* of the two cricketers: a significant phrase, given what was to happen in the High Court in 1977.

The biggest change in Australian cricket came with the staging of matches under lights. The second summer of World Series Cricket, in 1978-79, coincided with a traditional Ashes series, when Australia and England played six Tests, England winning the series 5–1. On November 28, 1978, just before the First Test, WSC Australia played a limited-overs match against WSC West Indies at the Sydney Cricket Ground, the first night-time cricket in this great arena. There were traffic jams approaching Moore Park and, by the dinner-break, more than 25,000 people were already in the ground. Kerry Packer then ordered the gates be thrown open. It was estimated by the ground authorities that more than 52,000 people watched the match, played in one of the more extraordinary and exciting atmospheres I have ever known.

New players were being signed by World Series Cricket for year three, and there was no doubt about the success of the organisation in the second season, after a slow start 12 months earlier. The new players meant that, in 1979-80, WSC's competition would have teams from Australia, West Indies, Pakistan and a World XI made up of Indian, English and South African cricketers.

Two things stand out. Packer started WSC on April 6, 1977, in his office in Sydney, and he ended it on February 13, 1979, when he flew to Adelaide and had morning tea in Bradman's Holden Street home. During an hour-long meeting, he set out an impressive list of WSC's plans for the future. He outlined the new players signed, the new tours to take place and confirmed burgeoning figures for day-night games and television ratings. His suggestion was that it was time for a settlement.

At the next Australian Board of Control meeting, Don is reported to have looked at all those present and said that before the meeting was concluded an agreement between the two parties would be on the table. And it all happened because of the tea and scones at Holden Street. It concluded the greatest revolution the game of cricket has known, and completely changed for the better the manner in which television covered all sports, not just cricket, for billions of people around the world. It also ensured that cricketers would in future receive proper financial reward for their skills.

Kerry Packer passed away on Boxing Day 2005... He was a remarkable man who changed for ever the manner in which cricket would be programmed, and at what time of the day, or night, it would take place.

Giants of the Game

*R*ichie Benaud was rarely more engaged, or engaging, *than when he spoke about the greats. Three of his most memorable contributions to* Wisden *were tributes to Australia's finest: Sir Donald Bradman, Keith Miller and Shane Warne.*

When Miller died in 2004, the Wisden *editor Matthew Engel asked Benaud to write an appreciation for the 2005 Almanack.* "He said yes," *wrote Engel in his* Financial Times *tribute to Benaud.* "I murmured something about the fee. He got quite cross: he did not want money; he would not accept money, not even a charitable donation on his behalf; this was an obligation that transcended money. I have never, ever had another conversation like that."

In his essay on Warne, written in 2000, Benaud was at his most prescient. "In fewer than 60 Tests [Glenn McGrath and Warne] have played together, they have taken 589 wickets for Australia. This is an astonishing statistic and it illuminates two things: that you need a partner at the other end; and that Australia might have problems when that combination breaks up."

A year later, on March 25, 2001, Benaud delivered a eulogy at the memorial service for Bradman. It was published in Wisden Cricketers' Almanack Australia

2001-02. *Bradman, he said, "had the most brilliant and incisive mind of anyone I have ever known in cricket".*

THE DON   Richie Benaud

It's not quite perfect outside, I guess. Rain coming down. A bit of a dodgy pitch. Wind blowing. But I reckon he would have handled it with all his consummate skill, no matter what it might provide out there.

There is a crowd out there filled with memories. The bowling changes here at the Cathedral End have been many and varied. We've now got an ageing leg-spinner, and I think The Don might have welcomed that.

He was the most famous of them all at a time when despair ruled Australia because of the Great Depression. Seventy years later 100 selectors from around the world nominated the five greatest players of the century [for *Wisden 2000*]. The Don received 100 votes. Not far away from him was that finest of all-rounders, Garry Sobers, who got 90. But 100 out of 100 is pretty good.

When I was six years old Bradman was captain of Australia in the concrete storeroom at Jugiong where I played Test matches. When I was ten he was still captain on the back verandah at Parramatta where he led and won and was absolutely brilliant in all those Test matches I used to play against England. I wasn't alone, in that thousands and thousands of other youngsters around Australia played their Test matches like that – Bradman and Stan McCabe made all the runs and then Bill O'Reilly and Clarrie Grimmett bowled out England every time. Wondrous days.

It wasn't just cricket. It was family too, and I'm very conscious of John and Shirley with their memories of their father. In recent sad times I'm conscious of the way in which Greta and Tom have talked of their grandparents, and with all of them their love and respect for a great lady in Jessie.

When he first came under notice as a cricketer he was playing such good tennis that there was some thought that he would have to make a decision. When he was chosen in the combined country side to go to Sydney the decision was made for him. Percy Westbrook, his boss at the time, said he could have a week off to do one or the other, but not both.

And a year or so later, when he was thinking of coming up to Sydney to play club cricket, my own club, which was then known as Central Cumberland, had the opportunity of signing him. Not with the same sort of fat contract you might get these days: we had to pay his train fare from Bowral to Sydney and back to Bowral. It was around four and sixpence, and quite correctly we decided that was far too expensive.

He was also a very good golfer. He shot his age for many years, but once he was dropped to B Grade at the club he played at in Adelaide. He made it known very quickly to the handicapper and to the chief executive of the club that he had never been B-grade at anything in his life. He won the silver medal the following week and was whizzed back up to A Grade.

I was lucky to be around as captain when that extraordinary series of Test matches was played against West Indies in 1960-61. One of the significant happenings in Australian cricket came about at the start of that series when, the night before the first day of the Tied Test, The Don came to me and asked if it would be all right if he came to speak to the team. Now this was a bit strange in those days. They called it protocol way back in 1960, and the players didn't know what it was all about. It was the first time it had ever happened.

The gist of his short talk was that he and Jack Ryder and Dudley Seddon, the other two selectors, would be looking in kindly fashion on those cricketers in Australia who played the game in attractive and attacking fashion and thought of the game rather than themselves. The unspoken words were that anyone not wanting to fit in with those plans shouldn't think about giving up their day job.

It was that vision as a selector that I found so outstanding and interesting. A classic example was early in 1963. The phone rang and it was Don on the other end. He said, "I have got a bit of news for you about your team for the last Test at the SCG. Neil Hawke is playing." I said, "What are you doing that for? Hawkey's quite a good prospect but has done nothing this year." He said, "I know that. And just in case he has an ordinary season next year we are giving him a Test under his belt because we have earmarked him to go to England in 1964." That is what I call vision.

Although he wrote very well on cricket, a variety of experiences over the years made him less than comfortable with journalists. He was certainly an unusual person in that regard, in that he guarded his privacy so much with the media. It was also unusual that he would be part of an Australian Cricket Board that chose a journalist to be their captain. In the early 1960s over a couple of glasses of red he expressed the thought that he and I seemed to be – "out of kilter" was his phrase – we were out of kilter in our relations with the press. That ideally he might have been better to have been more flexible in his time and I might have been better to have been slightly less so in my time.

His classic book *The Art of Cricket* managed to slice through the rhetoric of cricket coaching – no mean feat, I can tell you. It is also quite an achievement to have written a book which is just as good 40 years after it first rolled off the old-fashioned printing presses. When he was on tour in

America with Arthur Mailey's team the photograph was taken that is on the front page of the book.

The more important tour was the one he undertook in 1948. That was the one where he was captain of the "Invincibles", and some of those great cricketers are here tonight. He was always of the opinion that it was close to impossible, because of changes in conditions, to judge which was the best-ever cricket team. One thing we can be sure of, though, is that those Invincibles would have given more than a reasonable account of themselves in any contest against any other combination in any era. Three of those – Keith Miller and Arthur Morris and Ray Lindwall – were wonderful mentors for me. They did a superb job of trying to get me to think about the game and people and to do the right thing, all in their completely different ways.

Miller underlined for me the fact that it's a good thing never to take oneself too seriously. Back in 1950-51 Freddie Brown had the MCC side out here, and New South Wales were playing South Australia in Adelaide in the Shield game just before the First Test in Brisbane. It was November and as a selector Don was watching the match just 20 yards along to the right where the visitors' dressing-room was and still is. Phil "Pancho" Ridings gave us a most awful hammering that day – thrashed us everywhere. We were a very weary bunch at the end of the day, resting in the leather chairs and looking over here to the Cathedral, not saying much. Except I was chirping away. You've got to bear in mind that I had just turned 20 and I knew most of what there was to be known about cricket, so I chirped. I didn't get much response at first but I chirped again. I said to Miller that because Bradman had retired the moment I came into the game it was one of the sorrows of my life that I had never been able to bowl my leg-spinners to him. It was still very hot, about 85 to 90 degrees at that time of the day, and South Australia had just belted their way to four for 374. Nugget never took his eyes off the Cathedral. He didn't turn to me but just looked straight ahead and ruminated for a full two seconds before murmuring: "We all have one lucky break in our lives, son, and that could have been yours."

In the images of the family funeral a few weeks ago there were some memorable moments, sad but memorable. I was particularly taken by three things, which to me had a bearing on the fact that he was regarded with affection by old and young.

There were older people standing silently and just looking. There was a youngster, a boy scout, who saluted and held his salute. And then there was what a few people had said to me they thought to be a little irreverent, and that was "Aussie, Aussie, Aussie, oi, oi, oi!" Because he was a sportsman with such vision and because he had a feel for young cricketers – no one ever had a better feel for them; of all the people I have known he wanted to see youngsters get on – I think he would have liked the blending of the modern with the old in that moment with the funeral procession going past. It all marries into something that he used to talk about, that cricket simply is a reflection of life.

In Don's time he only wrote two major articles for *Wisden*. One was in 1939, the other in 1986. They were on precisely the same theme but with different words and at different lengths. They were along the lines that cricket needed to adapt to the quickening tempo of modern life. In the 1986 article he expressed his love for the traditional game, and had he still been with us he would have seen and applauded the magnificent short series recently concluded in India. He added a list of the good things about limited-overs cricket. That it rids the game of the unutterable bore who thinks occupancy of the crease and his own personal aggrandisement are all that matter. He talked of the outstanding fielding and running between the wickets of modern-day players in limited-overs cricket and now in Test cricket as well. He said it would seem logical in the future for cricket authorities to introduce arbitration from television cameras for some decisions. There was a lot of head-shaking about that. Some said it was absolute nonsense and would never happen. That was 15 years ago. It simply underlined the fact that he was still ahead of play. He had the most brilliant and incisive mind of anyone I have ever known in cricket.

Above all he was very much an Aussie. He was an Aussie sportsman and a great sportsman – said by his critics never once to have questioned an umpire's decision. He was a sportsman, and it wasn't just for a few sessions or a few days, it was for all eras and for all sports followers.

Above all else he was a sportsman.

Australia said farewell to another Invincible in 2004, when the daredevil all-rounder Keith Miller died at the age of 84. Benaud, who played with Miller, celebrated the life of a man who "managed to be a great cricketer and a star at the same time".

THE MAN WHO MADE CRICKET GLOW   Richie Benaud

Keith Miller's statistics – a Test bowling average just under 23, a batting average just below 37 – are maybe those of a very good cricketer, but not a great one. Those who look at them, examine them closely and then give something of a wave of the hand, miss the point in the way that some people now dismiss Victor Trumper. Trumper's batting average is ordinary compared to those who spend vastly more time at the crease, but much less time enthralling, entertaining, bemusing and imprinting themselves on the minds of cricket followers.

It was the same with Miller. In 1946 *Wisden* named him as the fastest bowler seen in England the previous summer. The war had just ended and the Victory Tests were played, and Miller was outstanding for the Australian Services' team with his prodigious hitting and innovative pace bowling. He became an overnight star in England, as he was to be in Australia after he returned and resumed playing Sheffield Shield. He became Australia's greatest all-round cricketer. To that you can add that he was also a much-loved character in both countries. His passing, on October 11, 2004, was an occasion for some sadness, but also for much raising of glasses to a man who captivated lovers of the game, not because of his statistics, but because he made cricket glow.

Miller was a one-off. I saw no one else in the time he played in Australian cricket who managed to be a great cricketer and a star at the same time. And that was without television, which began in Australia in 1956, the year he retired.

Everyone has heroes. Don Bradman was my first because, as a small boy, I listened on the giant-sized radio in Jugiong as he captained and turned around a 0–2 deficit to a 3–2 victory in the 1936-37 Ashes series. Then Clarrie Grimmett, because I saw him take six for 118 at the SCG in the first Sheffield Shield match I ever watched. After them it was Miller who, when playing for the Services against New South Wales, hit 105 off an attack which included Bill O'Reilly. Miller remained the hero even when I played in the same NSW and Australian side with him.

I was able to watch him at close quarters for the last six years of his career, and there were four things about him: skill, unpredictability, kindness and charisma. His skill, even when standing languidly at slip, was the reason young people do have heroes. As a batsman he made full use of his height and reach for the drive off both front and back foot. No one hit the ball harder. That didn't preclude him from the most delicate late cutting.

That mixture of grace and power was also the essence of his often devastating bowling. Miller's action was close to flawless, consisting of a wonderful delivery stride from a short run-up, his left arm high while looking over his left shoulder. He always had his bowling hand going in a full sweep past his left knee. He was genuinely fast, but also unorthodox in his thinking, always trying to stay two steps ahead of the batsmen. He had studied the art of swing by watching George Pope of Derbyshire and England, and there was no one who learned it better than Miller. With either bat or ball in hand, his thoughts were always attacking, a role model for any youngster watching either from the dressing-room or the Sydney Hill.

His approach to some matters, however, was less orthodox. In 1955-56 we twice played South Australia, the first time at the SCG and the second at the Adelaide Oval. In the Sydney match, Miller won the toss and then, bored with proceedings late in the day, closed our innings at 215 for eight. The South Australian openers successfully appealed against the light and "Nugget" was livid as he left the field. Also in our team was Peter Philpott. Like Miller, he lived in Manly, and Miller gave him a lift to the ground each morning. A few hours after that declaration, Miller's wife Peg gave birth to son Bob.

After a few celebratory drinks it was no wonder he was running late for the ground the next morning, and only remembered Philpott, standing on the Manly street corner, as he was speeding over the Harbour Bridge. Miller did a quick Jack Brabham U-turn, which was possible on the Bridge 50 years ago, and arrived at the SCG as I was very slowly, and rather reluctantly, leading the team on to the field in his absence. Somehow, he and Philpott made it in time, whereupon Miller, from the Paddington End, proceeded to take seven for 12 to bowl out South Australia for 27.

Twenty-five days later, in Adelaide, South Australia won the toss and batted. It was an action replay of Sydney, with Miller bowling so superbly that they were five down for 31, with left-hander Tim Colley, making his debut, yet to face a ball. Three wickets and 30 times past the outside edge were enough for Keith, and he decided the crowd should have a bit more batting entertainment. He had a casual look around the field and waved to Norman O'Neill, who was also making his Sheffield Shield debut.

"Come and have a bowl, Normie, Colley hasn't faced a ball in Shield cricket."

"I've never bowled one, Nug."

"Should be a good contest!"

It was an interesting debut for both of them. Colley made 57 but only played three games in his career. O'Neill didn't take a wicket and made a duck, then became one of Australia's finest batsmen. Miller was an outstanding captain, the finest never to have captained Australia in an era where speech-making and public relations sometimes rated above all else with the aptly named Australian Board of Control.

But his kindness was overwhelming. It covered everyone from those in prominent places to the guy who worked at the fishmonger's stall down the road from where he lived in London. Others away from sport were recipients: people he knew in both England and Australia who might have been down on their luck, or simply having a bad trot. It extended as well to young cricketers trying to make their way in the sporting world, and it was my personal good fortune to have as mentors Miller and his great friends, Arthur Morris and Ray Lindwall. For me, it was priceless luck that those three were here when I started in cricket.

He was sentimental too. Eight years ago I asked Nugget about the Victory Tests played when the war had just finished. The matches were fun, but sad as well because of those who weren't able to be there. He told me about one of the players, Graham Williams, the tall, broad-shouldered, bustling pace bowler, who was in the side having just been repatriated from a German prison camp after being shot down during the Libyan campaign. Williams had been four years in the camp and had spent most of that time teaching Braille to fellow prisoners, also to Germans blinded by the war.

Williams, as he walked slowly out to bat on the Lord's ground, looked around the 30,000 spectators, most of whom had read his harrowing story in the newspapers and heard it on the wireless over the past few days. He was still tall but there was nothing broad-shouldered about Williams that day. He was gaunt. Miller said he would never forget that instant when Williams came out to bat. Thirty thousand rose to their feet and clapped softly from the moment he appeared to the moment he reached the centre of the ground. The only sound to be heard was that soft, unbroken applause. "It was the most touching thing I have ever seen or heard, almost orchestral in its sound and feeling. Whenever I think of it, tears still come to my eyes."

It was on the same ground, in 1956, that Keith had his greatest match during a series which eventually produced more joy for Jim Laker and England than Australia. With Ray Lindwall and Alan Davidson injured and Pat Crawford, Lindwall's replacement, breaking down in his fifth over, Miller and Ron Archer had to do the fast-bowling job with the assistance of medium-pacer Ken Mackay. Everyone played a part in the match but Miller, aged 36, was simply magnificent. He bowled 70 overs from the Pavilion End and took ten for 152, one of the finest fast-bowling performances I have ever seen. He loved Lord's and he did it proud that day.

But it didn't matter whether he was in the action or not. He made the game come alive simply by being on the field. It is a rare gift. That is charisma, and that was Keith Miller.

In 2000, Shane Warne overtook Dennis Lillee as Australia's greatest wicket-taker. Benaud paid tribute in Wisden Cricketers' Almanack Australia 2000-01.

POSITIVE SPIN: THE RECORD-BREAKING SHANE WARNE
Richie Benaud

Among the many extraordinary things about Shane Warne, now Australia's leading Test wicket-taker, perhaps most remarkable is that he managed to play international cricket again after two critical and essential operations: to his spinning finger and his shoulder. Other cricketers have had injuries and recovered from them, but generally they were batsmen or pace bowlers. Inspiration and dedication is needed at these times. Warne's inspiration was Dennis Lillee who, 23 years earlier, went through hell mentally and physically to surmount severe back problems to get back on the field for Australia. Now other injured players in Australia, like Jason Gillespie and Damien Fleming, can look to Warne's example, so that even when told they might never make it back, they should not despair.

Warne's injuries were indisputably career-threatening. Two components an over-the-wrist spinner must have in perfect working order are his spinning finger and the rotator cuff of his shoulder. Each tiny part needs to work like well-oiled machinery; anything less, and the rusty arm, shoulder movement and body pivot conspire against the greatest effort.

It is a popular theory that the neck-stretching, back-cracking, hip-wrenching, knee-twisting golf swing is one of the most awkward movements performed by sports players. Yet Peter Thomson, in his memorable Rusacks Hotel interview with Henry Longhurst at St Andrews, managed to simplify it to three elements: put the club head in the correct position behind the ball, take the club head away and then hit the ball on the forward swing with the club face back in its original position. "Keep it simple" was his dictum. Over-the-wrist spinning is a little like that; you must keep it simple, as Warne does, and has done, on his way to becoming the greatest leg-spinner of his kind I have ever seen. Bill O'Reilly and Clarrie Grimmett, the other two great Australian spin bowlers, were different from each other and certainly different from Warne. That they didn't take as many wickets as Warne was because, in those days, Australia didn't play as many Tests; but it is noteworthy that when all three of them had played 27 Tests, covering the period of O'Reilly's Test career, the figures were Grimmett 147, O'Reilly 144 and Warne 124. Grimmett's figure of 216 wickets at the end of his career of 37 Tests is the most ever taken at that point of any bowler's career, fast or slow, so Warne is in very good company.

At times in recent history, the discipline of leg-spin has been threatened by administrative lethargy, fast-bowling domination and the shortened version of the game. The pet theory for quite a number of summers in limited-overs matches was that pacemen, all-rounders and quickish flat off-spinners are the only bowlers of interest to a captain and selectors. This assumed, however, that batsmen would suddenly and dramatically have improved their techniques against over-the-wrist spin, and off-spinners who had the gift of being able to flight the ball and spin it at the same time. It was loose thinking, and good bowlers of any type have proved able to hold their own in the game. Warne has been one of those, and his bowling in limited-overs internationals has often been outstanding, although it is unlikely that aspect would have had a great deal of influence on his being chosen as one of *Wisden*'s Five Cricketers of the Century. The fact that he was elected was a proper indication of the extraordinary impact he has had on the game of cricket in the relatively short time he has played.

Generally, bowlers come in pairs. Certainly this is often the case with fast bowlers: Gregory and McDonald, Lindwall and Miller, Lillee and Thomson for Australia; Trueman with Statham, Tyson with Statham and, in the West Indies, two pairs playing at once.

O'Reilly and Grimmett formed the outstanding Australian pairing of spin bowlers. Then, in Australia in the late 1950s, there was a different type of pairing involving Alan Davidson and me. From the time we first bowled together as the main bowlers in the Australian team at the Wanderers in Johannesburg, we took 333 wickets. We thought that was pretty good, until recently we looked at the modern-day pairing of Warne and Glenn McGrath. In fewer than 60 Tests they have played together, they have taken 589 wickets for Australia. *[McGrath and Warne ended*

with 1001 wickets from 104 Tests together.] This is an astonishing statistic, and it illuminates two things: that you need
a partner at the other end; and that Australia might have
problems in the near future when that combination breaks
up. Steve Waugh will be hoping he retains the services of
these two great bowlers for as long as possible. They have
formed one of the most important and, for opposition
batsmen, devastating combinations in the history of the
game. Coincidentally, Warne and McGrath each took 288
wickets in their first 62 Tests for Australia.

Warne on his way to 400 Test wickets has bowled out
teams, thought out batsmen, made captains happy and cost
opposition players their places in future teams. He has
lifted Australia on many occasions in the shortened game,
most notably in the World Cup of 1999, but also in the
previous one where the semi-final was played against West
Indies at Mohali. It was after that match I saw his swollen
blood-filled spinning finger and wondered how he had
been able to bowl at all, let alone bring Australia back from
a brink where West Indies had needed only 37 with eight
wickets in hand.

Warne has always desperately wanted to play for
Australia. That was so when he first played for Victoria, then
when he made his Test debut at the SCG in 1991-92; after
the World Cup in India, Pakistan and Sri Lanka and after his
shoulder operation. His chances of recovery from that
shoulder operation were considered minimal. As always
media people spent most of their waking moments, day and
night, trying to find something new to say about the issue.
There has never been any shortage of media feeding frenzies
with anything Warne does, but he will be remembered, in
the long term, more for the things he has done for Australian
cricket, especially how he changed the accent of youngsters,
so they wanted chiefly to bowl spin rather than pace.

When *Wisden*'s greatest five for the past 100 years were named early in 2000, there were many great players who missed selection. Those chosen from the past, Don Bradman, Jack Hobbs, Viv Richards and Garry Sobers, certainly qualify as great players. Warne is still playing and is a giant of the game.

Cricketers of the Year

*R*ichie Benaud completed a unique Wisden *double in 1962: he was named as one of the Five Cricketers of the Year (see page 8) and wrote an essay on another of the five, his team-mate Alan Davidson. "Davidson is a dynamic cricketer!" he said. "A superb left-hander with both bat and ball. Many of his exploits are legendary among his fellow modern-day players. New Zealand tourists tell of the match at Wairarapa where he took all ten wickets for 29 and then made a brilliant 160 not out to complete the day. The following game he relaxed by merely throwing out a scuttling batsman from the boundary with one stump at which to aim."*

In the 1970s he contributed essays on all six of the Australian Cricketers of the Year – four in 1973, after the thrilling 2–2 draw in the Ashes series the previous year, and two in 1976 after the inaugural World Cup. The list of subjects included the Chappell brothers and Dennis Lillee, and the usual Benaud themes emerge: total respect for what the man in the arena has been through and, in particular, a love of fast bowling – "to see [fast bowlers] scorching their way into the bowling crease is a matter of apprehension for the batsman and excitement for the spectator" – and attacking cricket. "If we are to believe the simple argument that the purpose of cricketers walking on to the field is to entertain," he wrote in 1973, "then no one more deserves the honour of being named one of the Five Cricketers of the Year than Keith Stackpole."

FIVE CRICKETERS OF THE YEAR 1962: ALAN DAVIDSON
Richie Benaud

When a cricketer can make 50 runs in a Test match he immediately becomes a valuable commodity to his side. When he has the ability to add to that five wickets and a brace of catches he is beyond price to his associates and skipper. Such a cricketer is ALAN KEITH DAVIDSON, born on June 14, 1929, of cricket-loving parents at Lisarow on the Central North Coast of New South Wales, and latterly one of the great all-rounders in the history of the game.

Davidson is a dynamic cricketer! A superb left-hander with both bat and ball. Many of his exploits are legendary among his fellow modern-day players. New Zealand tourists tell of the match at Wairarapa where he took all ten wickets for 29 and then made a brilliant 160 not out to complete the day. The following game he relaxed by merely throwing out a scuttling batsman from the boundary with one stump at which to aim.

... Who could care for statistics where there is concerned a player of the calibre of Davidson? Team-mates and spectators prefer to recall some of his paralysing bursts with the new ball for Australia, and the sight of his batting in full cry, preferably to some slow bowler. "When you see that big right foot coming down the wicket, brother, you duck," is an accurate and revealing recommendation given by an Australian bowler one day when asked how he felt about the carving just administered by the burly New South Welshman.

Like ten other Australians, one of his greatest moments in Test cricket was when he bowled Brian Statham to win the Ashes at Manchester in that fantastic Test of 1961. And rightly so, for without Davidson's magnificent 77 that day, Australians may well have been drinking their champagne from paper cups a couple of hours before the scheduled finishing time. That day the "big right foot" was well in evidence. Placed close to the line of the ball and with bat swinging majestically alongside it, he belted David Allen out of the attack – and Allen had just placed Mackay, Benaud and Grout in the pavilion for a paltry number of runs. One of the sixes which assisted a 20-run over flashed above cover's head; the next crashed against the brickwork alongside the railway line.

Every bit of 6ft and 14 stone went into those shots, in the same way it has gone into all that Davidson has done over the years for Australia. Over 1,000 runs, 162 wickets and nearly 50 close-to-the-wicket catches in Test matches give some idea why Australian players are prepared to argue about some of the "old-time greats" as compared with this player. The beauty of an almost perfect fast-medium action with a disconcerting late swing has caused untold worry to opening batsmen the world over.

Peter Richardson, Willie Watson and Tom Graveney will long recall the day he took three wickets for one run in a sensational over in the Second Test at Melbourne in 1958-59 – just as vividly others will remember a burst with the second new ball at Pietermaritzburg in 1957-58 when he whipped three Natal batsmen back to the pavilion in one over for no runs, among them Test player Roy McLean.

Thirty-nine Test matches for his country have brought the left-hander to the top of the cricketing tree, though for many of those he was playing in the shadow of the great Australian pair, Keith Miller and Ray Lindwall. It was not until these players were out of the side that Davidson came into his own.

In South Africa in 1957-58 he left batsmen foundering and critics advising as he savoured the delights of the new ball for the first time as an Australian bowler. England, in

1958-59; India and Pakistan, in 1959-60; and the West Indies, 1960-61, all felt the lash of his talents.

Indeed, one of his greatest performances was to take 33 wickets against the Caribbean visitors at a cost of 18 runs apiece when the next-best average was 33 per wicket and five of the West Indians scored over 350 in the Test matches.

Davidson has announced that he will not tour again with an Australian side, but with his fitness restored and some sterling performances against his name in the 1961-62 Sheffield Shield season, Australians are looking to him for a great season against England later this year, and justifiably so; for he has never let them down yet.

FIVE CRICKETERS OF THE YEAR 1973: GREG CHAPPELL

Richie Benaud

The Chappell brothers, Ian and Greg, are destined always to live with the shadow of their famous grandfather, the former Australian captain, Victor Richardson. The key words are "live with" rather than "live in", as happens with so many sportsmen who follow on from famous uncles, fathers or grandfathers. Ian and Greg are splendid Test cricketers in their own right and Greg Chappell, on the 1972 tour of England, confirmed his place as Australia's number one batsman.

He played two superb innings on the tour, the first at Lord's in the Second Test match where he made a magnificent 131, and the other at The Oval in the final Test where, after two Australian wickets had fallen for 34, he joined his brother in a wonderful 200-run partnership that steered Australia to around the 400 mark in their first innings.

Statistically, on the whole of the tour, Greg headed the Australian averages with 1,260 runs in 17 innings, hitting four centuries and three half-centuries.

But bare statistics hold little place in a summing up of those two Test innings. The one at Lord's can be rated alongside Bob Massie's bowling as the most vital performance in the whole game – a superbly judged piece of batting that, technically, was beyond reproach.

... GREGORY STEPHEN CHAPPELL was born on August 7, 1948, at Unley in South Australia, the second son of Martin and Jeanne Chappell – the latter the daughter of Victor Richardson. An early education at St Leonard's Primary School was followed by secondary school at Prince Alfred College in Adelaide. He joined the Glenelg Club whilst still at school in 1960, and has played for them ever since. His first Sheffield Shield match was for South Australia against Victoria in the 1966-67 season, under the captaincy of Les Favell who, in that game, hit 90 and 118 against the traditional Victorian rivals. This was while Greg's brother, Ian, was in South Africa with the Australian side, so the middle Chappell did not have the pleasure of making his debut with the older brother.

... There is a touch of irony in that all four Australians this year chosen by *Wisden* as Cricketers of the Year attribute at least part of their success to having had experience of English conditions. Dennis Lillee and Bob Massie give full credit to their stint in Lancashire and Scottish League cricket, Keith Stackpole does the same for his batting experience in the Lancashire League, and Greg Chappell was one of the best players with Somerset in the 1968 and 1969 seasons.

Greg Chappell, least of the quartet, had to make any drastic change of technique because of his time in county cricket and, as the 1972 tour went on, so did he improve in strokeplay and stature. "I did not have to make any great changes but I think the key to it all was that a change did develop over the period I was with Somerset. At the same time, there were still things I had to improve on by the time I got across to England in 1972, particularly with the damp start to the season, which meant the medium-pace bowlers were cutting the ball off the pitch a considerable amount. It wouldn't be true to say I had to make any drastic changes but I am certainly grateful for the experience I gained with Somerset for those two years."

... There was a time when Greg Chappell was so strong on the on side that it was considered poor form not to concentrate round about his off stump and induce the edged chance to the wicketkeeper or slip. In the space of 12 months, all that has changed. Critics watching his performance against the Rest of the World in the international matches in 1971-72 compared him favourably with some of the great players over the years in Australian first-class cricket. The subsequent tightening of his technique in the England tour leaves few in any doubt that, for some years, he is going to be the outstanding batsman in Australia.

He has also his medium-pace bowling to sway the selectors, if ever they might be in any doubt about his inclusion, but these days he bowls less and less. He still has the ability to break through the partnership, but the concentration now is on batting and fielding, and in the latter department he has no peer in Australia, either in close catching positions or away from the wicket...

He is one of the new young breed of Australian cricketers who have the intense desire to see Australia back on top in international cricket. His first experience of Test cricket was to be in a losing side in a series against England, and this at the end of a disastrous five years of Australian cricket. Chappell has been part of the fightback in a team well led by his brother and with a younger brother coming along in splendid fashion in Australian first-class cricket at present. It could well be a family affair by the time England next come to Australia.

FIVE CRICKETERS OF THE YEAR 1973: DENNIS LILLEE
Richie Benaud

The Haslingden club in the Lancashire League has a lot to answer for in the emergence of Dennis Lillee as Australia's trump card in the 1972 tour of England. Lillee, who is not yet at his peak, should be in even better bowling form when the England side comes to Australia next year, and he gives full credit to the season he had in Lancashire. "I think it was probably one of the real turning points in my career. It certainly forced me to become more accurate and learn a little bit about bowling, rather than merely thump down the ball as fast as possible. Quite often in the league games, footholds would be too slippery to bowl really fast, and accuracy and movement off the pitch would be the prime requirements. Now this couldn't have come at a better time as, up to that stage, I'd been concentrating solely on pace."

Not too many English spectators will hold it against the Lancashire League club that they had a hand in the emergence of Lillee as a fine fast bowler on that tour. He definitely added excitement to the game of cricket, if one can excuse the problem of perhaps too long a run to the crease. But, in keeping with other great fast bowlers like Ray Lindwall, Frank Tyson and Wes Hall, the long run is inclined to add to the excitement. The dull thing is to watch a medium-pacer take too long a run – to see some of the players named above, scorching their way into the bowling crease, is a matter of apprehension for the batsman and excitement for the spectator.

DENNIS KEITH LILLEE was born at Subiaco, Perth, on July 18, 1949, and, after attending Belmay Primary School and Belmont Secondary School, he began playing with the Perth Cricket Club when 15 years of age. Four years later, he made his debut against Queensland at Brisbane, capturing the wicket of the very experienced opening batsman, Sam Trimble, as his first victim in first-class cricket. It was a moderate debut by the then slimly built West Australian, for he took two for 60 in the first innings and one for 16 in the second. But, from that point on, he could do nothing wrong.

Australia had been looking for a fast bowler ever since the retirement of that great left-hander, Alan Davidson... 1970-71 was the Australian year of fast bowlers – for England anyway. John Snow, Bob Willis and Peter Lever gave the Australians a torrid time and, with the Third Test match at Sydney going to England by a mammoth 299 runs and the Fifth in Melbourne being drawn, the Australian selectors decided to make changes for the Sixth Test at Adelaide. To do this, they put in Lillee, and he repaid them by taking five wickets in the first innings and going on to take another three wickets in the final Test match played at Sydney, a game also won by England.

... When the South African tour of Australia was cancelled in 1971-72, a series against the Rest of the World XI was put on in its place and Lillee, in the opening game at Brisbane, gave the first indication of the big advance his bowling had made in the off season. Although his figures were one for 73 and two for 38, his more compact run to the crease and much better control impressed sound judges at the Gabba over the five days of that game. He was more confident in his approach to the opposing batsmen and, when the second representative game came along in Perth on December 10, 1971, Australians, for the first time since Davidson, were able to welcome a new fast-bowling star.

The match was scheduled for five days but lasted only three. The World XI side made just 59 in their first innings, Lillee taking eight for 29, and then he chipped in with four for 63 in the second innings, allowing Australia to win by an innings and 11 runs.

Lillee marks this down as his most memorable game of cricket. "I felt shocking when I got to the ground – some sort of virus was going around Perth at the time – and, after bowling a couple of overs for the wickets of Sunil Gavaskar and Farokh Engineer, I felt terribly tired and asked Ian Chappell if I could possibly have a rest. He talked me into having one more over, and things suddenly began to happen after Graham McKenzie dismissed Rohan Kanhai and Zaheer Abbas was run out. I think that was the most memorable match I've played in from a personal performance point of view, but the best bowling experience I've had was in the final Test at The Oval [in 1972], where we just had to win that match to square the series... It was a really hard grind on a beautiful batting pitch that gave a little bit of assistance to the pace bowlers if they were prepared to put a bit into it, and I finished up bowling 56 overs in the game. It would have been nice to put my feet up after that without any worries but we still had to make nearly 250 to win the game and square the rubber and it was one of the most nerve-wracking innings I've watched."

"... It really was a marvellous tour for us and it's a great feeling to know you've been part of something that has perhaps made cricket more popular or helped the game as far as the public is concerned, and it was wonderful to see the big crowds at every Test match over there. I'm not sure though that I agree a drawn series was a fair result. I feel we were the better side and, given a good cricket pitch, instead of the one we had at Headingley, I think we'd be holding the Ashes now."

... In the Test series, Lillee did a magnificent job for his skipper, Ian Chappell, bowling 250 overs and breaking the Australian wicket-taking record for a series against England with 31 victims. His long hair flying and his features adorned with a moustache in the best tradition of old-time cricketers, such as Fred Spofforth, he always posed a problem, even for the best of England's batsmen...

Though he looks flamboyant in action on the field, Lillee is essentially a man of simple character, preferring a king-size steak to the more spicy continental dishes, and the occasional glass of beer to a magnum of champagne... On the field a man who shows an obvious dislike to batsmen, he is of equable temperament once the day's play is over, and the only thing he is prepared to dislike in cricket at the moment is the type of field set for him in one-day cricket fixtures on the England tour. "There was one occasion where they even wanted to take my slip away," he said. "When that happens, it's almost time to give the game away."

The least comforting thing for England's batsmen is that Lillee should be right at his peak when England arrive in Australia on the next occasion and he should still be in good bowling form in 1977 when at the age of 28, he accompanies the next Australian team to England.

FIVE CRICKETERS OF THE YEAR 1973: BOB MASSIE
Richie Benaud

It needed no crystal ball to deduce that the greatest cricket match in Bob Massie's life was the Lord's Test in 1972 when his own personal contribution of 16 wickets gave Australia a magnificent victory and squared the series at that point. It was a doubly pleasant experience for Massie, for it was his first Test match… Two or three years before, he had been rejected by Northamptonshire after he had been offered a trial at a time when he was playing as a professional in the Scottish League with Kilmarnock. Who knows? Had Northamptonshire recognised the talent in Massie and taken him on a three-year contract, Australia might well have been two down after that Lord's Test. Certainly it was an extraordinary match in what turned out later to be one of the best Test series ever played between England and Australia.

… In the Massie family, Christian names are the vogue – Bob's father is Arnold Joseph George William Massie. A Perth chiropodist, he and his wife Barbara called their son, born on April 14, 1947, ROBERT ARNOLD LOCKYER MASSIE. The younger Massie began playing cricket when he was ten at the Bedford Park Youth Club, when he was attending the Hill Crest Primary School. Later he was to go to Mount Lawley Senior High School in the years from 1959 to 1963 and he joined Bassendean-Bayswater as his first step into Western Australian club cricket. To his team-mates he is known as "Fergie", a shortening of Massey-Ferguson, the tractor people, and the "Fergie" comes from the second part of the name – all very complicated but it passes the time in the dressing-room!

Massie rolled over the England batsmen in that Lord's Test match almost as though he was using a tractor rather than a sphere of hard red leather. Although that game rates definitely as the most memorable match in which he has ever played – his first Test – he doesn't list it as necessarily his best bowling. Rather he inclines to the game between Australia and the Rest of the World in Sydney in the 1971-72 season, when he believes he got himself a trip to England by taking seven for 76 in 20.6 overs. It was just prior to this that Garry Sobers had played his astonishing innings of 254 in the third international in Melbourne, a match in which Dennis Lillee took eight wickets and Massie himself took three. He believes it was important that he came back in the next fixture to grab those seven wickets, one of which was Sobers, dismissed by a perfectly pitched off-cutter that moved away from the left-hander.

... Only two bowlers on the 1972 tour of England bowled over 400 overs, Lillee and Ashley Mallett, and Massie bowled 382 in all first-class matches, reaching his 50th wicket at the end of the tour. In Tests he took 23 wickets at an average of 17, twice taking five in an innings and once ten in a match – those figures relate to the extraordinary performance at Lord's.

Cricket followers should keep Massie's Lord's performance in perspective, however, and not expect too much too soon from him... success, in fact, has come very quickly for Massie, and it would be unwise, apart from applauding, to pay too much attention to his one sensational performance in that Lord's Test. He is basically a good young bowler, and one who will get better and better as he gains in experience, and the most important part of his tour of England was not that he took 16 wickets in a Test but that he fulfilled the selectors' hopes in that he improved steadily and went back to Australia a better bowler. He knows quite well that there is lot of hard slog ahead of him but he is a very hard worker and a deep thinker on bowling. His idea of bowling round the wicket to the England batsmen in the Lord's Test was devised at Old Trafford where, for hours each day, he bowled in that style to his team-mate Ross Edwards in the nets at the back of the ground.

It could well be that Massie needs the experience of another tour to the West Indies, where line and length will play such a big part in his bowling, and it will not be surprising if he is not really at his peak until the England side comes to Australia on the next occasion.

FIVE CRICKETERS OF THE YEAR 1973: KEITH STACKPOLE
Richie Benaud

If we are to believe the simple argument that the purpose of cricketers walking on to the field is to entertain, then no one more deserves the honour of being named one of the Five Cricketers of the Year than KEITH RAYMOND STACKPOLE, the Australian opening batsman, born at Collingwood, a suburb of Melbourne, on July 10, 1940.

There were some, the England players included, who believed by the time the 1972 Test series was over that Stackpole was batting with a magic wand rather than an ordinary sliver of willow. Every so often he managed to get an outside edge to an attempted cut or drive and, in more cases than not, the ball flew clear of the field. Some of the opposition regarded this as lucky, but I think it would be true to say the spectators watching the game at the ground or on television may well have thought themselves to be the fortunate ones instead of Stackpole. Anyone paying his money to watch a game of cricket would always forgive a little bit of luck going the way of the man who continually tries to entertain.

Stackpole was 31 years of age when he made his first tour of England – perhaps a little late for a man to take his first tilt at England's top bowlers on their own pitches. But he had been in the Australian side since 1965-66, when he played against M. J. K. Smith's team in Adelaide, and had steadily matured, first of all as a middle-order batsman and then as a dashing opener.

Certainly if family ties have anything to do with success in cricket, Stackpole was destined to have a sound future in the game. His father, also Keith Stackpole, was very much of the build and attacking disposition of his son, who later was to go further in the game than did his mentor. Keith senior was a top-line player in Victoria, where he played in the Sheffield Shield team at a time when it was very strong, and both father and son batted in much the same vein, concentrating mainly on cutting and hooking. In recent times, the younger Stackpole has matured his game and become a very strong driver, playing much more off the front foot than he did when he first came into the Australian side.

As a boy he attended St John's Clifton Hill Primary School and then moved on to the Christian Brothers' College, Clifton Hill, where he began to excel at the game. Having seen his father play in first-class cricket, and now his father having the privilege of watching his son play for Australia, there is no doubt that the younger Stackpole has modelled himself on Keith senior.

At Collingwood, his Melbourne club, he came under the eagle eye of Jack Ryder, Victorian and Australian selector and former Australian captain, who was one of the strongest drivers the game has known. Jack, a most astute judge of a cricketer, was always keen to see a batsman standing upright and hitting the ball straight down the ground off either back or front foot, but he wasn't able to instil in Stackpole the overwhelming desire to play this stroke. Instead, when Stackpole made his debut for Victoria against South

Australia in the 1962-63 Australian season, his reputation listed him as being a very strong player off the back foot, round about the point and square-leg area, and a more than useful change bowler as well as a good slip field.

… At the age of 32 [Stackpole's birthday was during the England tour] he was one of the oldest players in the Australian side last year but he has plenty of cricket left in him, both for Australia and Victoria. What looks from the grandstand a fairly open batting method proved successful enough on English pitches, despite a school of thought that Stackpole may have had some difficulty because of his concentration on back-foot strokes…

Although Stackpole is the essence of modesty about his own performances, he is correctly regarded by team-mates and cricket followers as being as close to an ideal member of a touring team as one could find. He is very helpful with young players, has the fierce will to win so necessary in international cricket, and is one of the most regular workers in the practice nets. He topped the Australian batting aggregate on the England tour, hit five half-centuries and one century and, as well, made most runs on the tour in first-class matches, being beaten in the averages only by Greg Chappell.

Few people enjoy playing cricket more than Stackpole, and only one aspect of the game causes him concern these days. "I am afraid I am rather disillusioned about one-day cricket," he said. "I know it is extremely popular in England and is definitely part of the game there, and it is our job to play the matches which are put on the programme. To me though, one-day knockout cricket should be attractive and yet most of it seems to be played in defensive vein. The one thing I would like to see happen in the game is that some way should be found to have these one-day fixtures played in an attacking manner."

He is able to speak from strength on that issue, for few more attacking cricketers have appeared at international level in the past 25 years.

FIVE CRICKETERS OF THE YEAR 1976: IAN CHAPPELL

Richie Benaud

Australian cricket was going through a disastrous period when IAN MICHAEL CHAPPELL was thrust into the captaincy in the final Test of the 1970-71 series against England. He lost his first Test by 62 runs, his second by 89 runs – and then was never beaten in a Test series against any country. When Chappell took over, the national team had not won a Test in the previous nine times of asking. To make room for him at the top, the Australian selectors removed W. M. Lawry in a step that had all the subtlety of the guillotine in the French Revolution...

When Chappell took over as captain the bowling attack was an inexperienced Dennis Lillee, Tony Dell from Queensland, Doug Walters, Greg Chappell, Terry Jenner and Kerry O'Keeffe. It was not until the Second Test in England at Lord's in 1972 that the Lillee–Massie combination came together and they squared the series there, with Bob Massie making a dream debut in Test cricket.

Back in Australia two names were on the selectors' short list for the future; Jeff Thomson and Max Walker, the first an unorthodox but very fast bowler and the second a promising medium-pacer. It was on those two, plus Lillee and the reliable Ashley Mallett, that Chappell based his on-the-field strategy, and Australia have not had many better combinations over the years with the ball, particularly when allied to the brilliant close catching produced by the team. The fast bowlers' skills were blunted a little by the dry summer in England in 1975, but Chappell still won that series and, in the final Test at The Oval, announced his decision not to be available again to captain Australia.

Chappell captained Australia 30 times, won 15 of those games and lost only five, two of the latter being his first two efforts. By the time he retired from the leadership to be a Test player only he had lifted Australia right back to the top in world cricket. His brother Greg took over the captaincy and celebrated his appointment by becoming only the fourth Australian to hit a century in his first innings as skipper – 123 against West Indies in Brisbane.

Ian left him a legacy of a very good cricket team with a wonderful team spirit and a burning ambition to stay on top. He did more than that, however, for his players. Ian Chappell is and was very definitely a players' man. He has had more brushes with officialdom than any other players since Keith Miller and Sidney Barnes just after the end of the war, and most of those brushes have been because of his unwillingness to compromise.

Nothing is a shade of grey to Chappell and, although his candid speech and honesty can be refreshing, the same attributes also have landed him in trouble with administrators on several occasions... Chappell himself would disclaim any suggestion of militant-shop-steward-style thinking but he has certainly livened things up in four years of captaincy, in a game where the top players have always been ridiculously underpaid.

At the same time, he has batted brilliantly for Australia on many occasions and is approaching 5,000 runs in Tests. The man he succeeded as captain, Bill Lawry, classes him as Australia's best player on all types of pitches, a rating that is disputed by those who see his brother Greg as one of the great players for Australia since the war. As batsmen they are different types, as different as they are in personality. Greg is the more elegant strokeplayer of the pair, Ian the more rugged and ebullient in his shotmaking.

Ian was born on September 29, 1943 at Unley, South Australia, and played first for South Australia against Tasmania in the 1961-62 season, hit a splendid century against New South Wales a little later and played in the only Test against Pakistan in Melbourne in 1964. In 1965-66 in Australia, he played in the final two Tests when Australia squared the Ashes series, but his Test batting results were moderate until he played against India in Melbourne in December 1967 and hit a magnificent 151 against an attack based on spin.

In 1968 in England, he finished second in the Test averages to Lawry, averaging 43 for 348 runs, and he topped the tour batting figures with 1,261 runs at 48.50 per innings – Ian Redpath was the only other batsman to reach 1,000 runs for the tour. After being made captain he played some splendid fighting innings for Australia, notably in the opening Test in Brisbane in 1974-75 when, on a pitch of decidedly variable bounce, he made 90 and allowed Australia to finish with a first-innings score of 309. In England in 1975, he had a great series, scoring 429 runs at 71.50 and making 192 at The Oval, as well as three other half-centuries.

He has been a most reliable No. 3 for his country – never backward in taking on the fast bowlers with the hook shot, though in recent times he has been more careful to pull in front of square leg rather than hook in the area behind the umpire. His batting technique has been carefully planned to provide the best possible returns against pace bowling and he is always concentrating on getting behind the line of the ball, too much so on occasions when England's fast bowlers have been able to take advantage of a sight of the leg stump.

He hit a century in his final match as captain of Australia, and his brother Greg, who was one of the *Wisden* Five in 1973, hit a century in his first Test as Australian captain. A unique record. The statistics will not unduly delight Ian… he is interested more in winning cricket matches than in the figures produced by those who do the winning.

FIVE CRICKETERS OF THE YEAR 1976: RICK MCCOSKER
Richie Benaud

Over the years Australia has a solid record of cricketers who have graduated from country areas to the city, on to Sheffield Shield cricket and then into the Test arena. The most famous of them was Don Bradman, who hit 118 in his initial Sheffield Shield game against Clarrie Grimmett; then there was Stan McCabe and, since then, many boys from the bush have moved on to greater things. In New South Wales in recent years Brian Booth and the left-arm spinner Johnny Martin are two who were taught their cricket in the country. Booth later moved to Sydney to live, but Martin continued to live at Burren Creek and journey to Sydney each week to play club cricket.

Following in their cricketing footprints is RICHARD BEDE McCOSKER. Born on December 11, 1946, he played his early cricket in his native Inverell – a country town 418 miles from Sydney and closer to Brisbane than to the southern city. McCosker is anything but the prototype of the young shooting star. He was 20 years of age when he made the move to Sydney, where he joined a grade club as a third grader! By the end of that season he was in first grade, but his main worry then was whether or not he could hold his place in that grade the following summer. It took him five seasons to catch the eye of the New South Wales selectors at a time when NSW batting strength was at a low ebb.

... In New South Wales not many cricketers make their debut as batsmen within a fortnight of turning 27, but McCosker did it on November 23, 1973. In a way he struck a blow for late-maturing cricketers, the ones who need time to settle in, as distinct from the ones the selectors try to produce from nowhere.

His debut was less than auspicious. Terry Jenner's top-spinner accounted for him when he had made 13 in the first innings; he didn't bat a second time, and there was the anguish of wondering if he were to be given a second chance batting at No. 6. The following week he made 71 not out against Western Australia in Sydney, and he finished the season with 263 runs at 44 per innings, second only to Ian Davis of those who had made 250 runs for the summer.

At the age of 27 he had made it and, with England to tour Australia the next season, he must have forced himself on to a list of a dozen or so young players whom the selectors would be keeping an eye on...

[McCosker] could hardly have [made] a worse start to the [1974-75] season. Mike Denness's men were loosening up at the nets in Adelaide, whilst McCosker scored nine runs in two innings in Brisbane. Then shortly after, in Sydney, he chased 422 runs on the first day of the game against Western Australia, with Wally Edwards, Bruce Laird and Rod Marsh all hitting centuries.

There is not the slightest question in my mind that the second day of this match was the most vital in McCosker's cricket career. Before he had scored he was dropped at slip by John Inverarity off Dennis Lillee, a happening that brought an exclamation from Lillee which could be heard by people boating in the Kippax Lake. McCosker was undeterred. He batted calmly and courageously to steer New South Wales to 290 for five, remaining unbeaten with 138, but was dismissed next morning without adding to his score. New South Wales followed on and at 124 for five they were close to defeat, but McCosker hit another century, not out this time.

I watched both those innings from the press box and it was clear that here was a batsman of ability. He wasn't captivating to look at but he was a neat strokeplayer. He wasn't all that elegant but he was a fine timer of the ball. He wasn't dynamic but he was courageous and thoughtful for his batting partners. Above all, he tried tremendously hard and, in the end, New South Wales escaped their impending outright defeat.

When Western Australia's Wally Edwards was found out by the England fast bowlers in the first three Tests, the selectors gambled with McCosker for the Fourth in Sydney and he rewarded them with a fine innings of 80. In a short time he had moved from an inexperienced No. 6 for New South Wales to a Test opening batsman – quite a meteoric rise, even by Australian standards.

… McCosker's great season had the natural follow-up of selection for the Prudential World Cup and the four Tests against England and, again, he was an instant success. He is the first to admit however that English pitches in 1975 hardly posed the problems he had been told about by experienced players…

McCosker, as quiet and modest off the field as he is on it, has not thought about his prospects of captaincy but he took over New South Wales last season when Doug Walters was injured before the First Test against the West Indies. He did a sound, orthodox job and I would not be at all surprised if he fills a position of responsibility in the Australian team in years to come. He looks a ready-made deputy for Greg Chappell for the 1977 tour of England, a far cry from the struggles to gain recognition in the "big smoke" for five years from 1967.

Season By Season

*R*ichie Benaud made his first-class debut for New South Wales on December 31, 1948, in a Sheffield Shield match against Queensland. He played as a No. 6 batsman, making two in his only innings, and did not bowl.

This chapter is a record of Benaud's Test and first-class career, with all reports taken from Wisden Cricketers' Almanack between 1951 and 1965. The reports have been edited, with a focus on personal highlights; as such, they get longer as Benaud's slow-burning career progresses.

His first mention in Wisden came in the Overseas Cricket section of the 1951 Almanack, in the report of a Shield match between New South Wales and Victoria in December 1949. Benaud hit 68 in the first innings.

———

1949–50

Two 19-year-old batsmen, Jim Burke and Richie Benaud, rescued New South Wales with a fifth-wicket stand of 138 runs added in 135 minutes.

1951–52

Benaud made his maiden century against the South Africans in December 1951, helping New South Wales to win the match on first innings.

When the first four New South Wales wickets fell for 90 runs, Benaud, whose 117 included two sixes and 12 fours, turned the scales in a very fine display.

A month later, he made his Test debut in the final match of Australia's 4–1 victory over West Indies.

Australia v West Indies
Fifth Test Match, at Sydney, January 25–29, 1952
Australia 116 (G. E. Gomez 7-55) and **377;**
West Indies 78 (K. R. Miller 5-26) and **213** (J. B. Stollmeyer 104;
R. R. Lindwall 5-52).
Australia won by 202 runs.
Benaud: 3 and 19; did not bowl and 1-14.

When they dismissed Australia for a seemingly insignificant total on the first day it looked as though West Indies would succeed, but again their batting broke down against the Australian "bumper" attack, and this led to their heaviest reverse of the series. Seven wickets went down after lunch [on the fourth day] while only 24 runs were scored, and when Benaud claimed his first Test wicket by bowling Valentine the series was over.

1952–53

A year later Benaud played four of five Tests against South Africa, though his impact was modest: 124 runs and ten wickets.

AUSTRALIA 2–2 SOUTH AFRICA

Rarely in the history of international cricket has a team so thoroughly routed the prophets as did the young and markedly inexperienced side, led by J. E. Cheetham, which made South Africa's third visit to the Antipodes so momentous. Unquestionably, South Africa's achievement in winning two Tests and sharing the rubber provided the biggest cricket shock for many years.

Australia v South Africa

Second Test Match, at Melbourne, December 24–30, 1952

South Africa 227 and 388 (W. R. Endean 162*);

Australia 243 (H. J. Tayfield 6-84) and **290** (H. J. Tayfield 7-81).

South Africa won by 82 runs.

Benaud: 5 and 45; 2-20 and 0-23.

South Africa's first victory over Australia for 42 years came as reward for superior all-round cricket. Endean and Tayfield played specially notable roles, but the whole side deserved praise for two fielding performances which drew favourable comparison with some of the best teams of the past.

The last three days went all in favour of South Africa. A ninth-wicket stand of 61 by Benaud and the hard-hitting Ring temporarily raised Australia's hopes, but Tayfield split the stand and clinched South Africa's triumph.

Australia v South Africa

Third Test Match, at Sydney, January 9–13, 1953

South Africa 173 and 232;

Australia 443 (R. N. Harvey 190).

Australia won by an innings and 38 runs.

Benaud: 0; dnb and 2-21.

After their victory at Melbourne, South Africa entered this match not only on terms of equality but with the confidence which that success had given the players. Yet any hopes they held of succeeding again were virtually dispelled during the first two days when Australia established an overwhelming advantage.

Australia v South Africa
Fourth Test Match, at Sydney, January 24–29, 1953
Australia 530 (A. L. Hassett 163, C. C. McDonald 154) and **233-3 dec**
(R. N. Harvey 116);
South Africa 387 (W. A. Johnston 5-110) and **177-6.**
Drawn.
Benaud: 6 and 18; 4-118 and 1-28.*

After narrowly avoiding the follow-on, South Africa were set to make 377 in four and a quarter hours and they forced a draw, which enabled them to retain a chance of ending the series on level terms.

Australia v South Africa
Fifth Test Match, at Melbourne, February 6–12, 1953
Australia 520 (R. N. Harvey 205) and **209** (E. R. H. Fuller 5-66);
South Africa 435 (W. A. Johnston 6-152) and **297-4.**
South Africa won by six wickets.
Benaud: 20 and 30; 0-55 and 1-41.

South Africa gave one of the finest performances of their history, and the victory meant that for the first time in a series between the countries the honours were shared. Midway through this vital match South Africa's chances of saving defeat, let alone winning, did not look bright, but all-round skill rather than individual efforts enabled them to emerge victorious.

1953

The slow start to Benaud's Test career continued in his first Ashes series, when he averaged just three with the bat and 87 with the ball. But there were signs of his abundant talent in some of the tour games, most notably when he equalled a world record by smashing 11 sixes in an innings.

ENGLAND 1–0 AUSTRALIA
Norman Preston

After having held the Ashes for 19 years, the longest period on record, Australia surrendered them at The Oval where after four drawn Tests England won the fifth and last in convincing fashion by eight wickets. If the winning of Test matches were the only thing that mattered, then the team which Lindsay Hassett brought to Great Britain in 1953 did not carry out its mission. That was very far from the truth.

Rarely has any series of matches produced such interesting and exciting cricket. Day after day and sometimes hour and hour the pendulum swung first towards Australia and then towards England... The Australians' ambition was to enjoy their cricket. In this respect they provided a lesson for many English county cricketers. Naturally the Tests were their main consideration but as soon as the tension was over they gave some magnificent displays of hitting, culminating in that thrilling victory in their last important match at Scarborough, where Richie Benaud hit 11 sixes in his wonderful 135.

With their seniors failing it was not surprising that the strangers to England – Graeme Hole, Jim de Courcy, Alan Davidson and Benaud – fell easy prey when Alec Bedser and his fellow bowlers were in the full flush of success, but enough was seen of these youngsters to make one realise that the experience they gained on this tour may well help them to become better players as they mature. Indeed, I shall be surprised if a lot more is not heard of the three all-rounders, Davidson, Ron Archer and Benaud.

Turning to the bowling there was an appreciable weakness due to the absence of top-class spin. None of the three leg-spinners, Doug Ring, Jack Hill and Benaud, was seen to advantage in the Tests.

The Australian XI played four matches en route to England. In one, against a Combined XI, Benaud hit 167 not out and took seven wickets in the match – including the first five-wicket haul of his first-class career. A week later he struck an unbeaten hundred against Western Australia. When Australia arrived in England, he demolished Yorkshire with bat and ball.

Benaud was more forceful [than Miller], his 97, made in two hours, including four sixes and 11 fours… the leg-breaks of Benaud caused chief trouble. His analysis of seven for 46 was the best of his career.

England v Australia
First Test Match, at Nottingham, June 11–16, 1953
Australia 249 (A. L. Hassett 115; A. V. Bedser 7-55) and **123**
(A. V. Bedser 7-44);
England 144 (R. R. Lindwall 5-57) and **120-1.**
Drawn.
Benaud: 3 and 0; dnb and 0-15.

So stirring was the cricket of the first three days that the anticlimax brought about by prolonged bad weather aroused bitter disappointment. The consequences of the weather break must have been particularly galling to Bedser.

He was England's hero, with a match analysis of 14 wickets for 99 runs… Benaud made excellent catches from Graveney, at short leg, and Hutton, from a forcing stroke to gully.

England v Australia

Second Test Match, at Lord's, June 25–30, 1953

Australia 346 (A. L. Hassett 104; A. V. Bedser 5-105) and **368**

(K. R. Miller 109);

England 372 (L. Hutton 145; R. R. Lindwall 5-66) and **282-7**

(W. Watson 109).

Drawn.

Benaud: 0 and 5; 1-70 and 1-51.

In its swift changes of fortune the cricket followed a pattern similar to that of the Nottingham Test, except that here the suspense continued to the last over of the fifth day. Yet everything in the first four days paled before England's last-ditch stand which brought them a draw as stirring as the majority of victories.

Without detracting from the merit of Watson, Bailey or Compton, the Australian slow bowlers did not make the best use of a pitch from which the ball could be turned sharply.

Benaud was omitted for the drawn Third Test at Old Trafford before returning at Headingley.

England v Australia

Fourth Test Match, at Leeds, July 23–28, 1953

England 167 (R. R. Lindwall 5-54) and **275;**

Australia 266 (A. V. Bedser 6-95) and **147-4.**

Drawn.

Benaud: 7 and did not bat; 0-12 and 0-26.

Australia were always on top in this match and only by pursuing a policy of steadfast defence did England escape defeat The way was left clear for a straight contest for the Ashes in the Fifth Test at The Oval, to which both boards of control decided to add an extra day in the hope of reaching a definite conclusion.

Benaud was left out of the deciding Test. The pitch took spin, and England's Jim Laker and Tony Lock shared nine second-innings wickets to steal the match and series. The tour ended on a high for Benaud, however, when he equalled the then-world record by striking 11 sixes in an innings against T. N. Pearce's XI at Scarborough.

The Australians won by two wickets after three days of wonderful cricket by two teams each of which included ten men who had taken part in the Tests. The match produced 34 sixes and, crowning all, was the feat of Benaud in the fourth innings when he put his side on the path to victory by making 135 out of 209 in one hour 50 minutes. He hit 11 sixes and nine fours. Benaud went to 99 by hooking Bedser for six. A single gave him his first hundred in England, and then he launched a terrific attack. Scoring 25 in one over from Tattersall, he pull-drove the first four balls each for six and then in the following over was caught in the deep.

1953–54

There were no home Tests for Australia in 1953-54, which allowed Benaud to focus on domestic cricket. He was New South Wales's leading run-scorer (665) and wicket-taker (30) during another triumphant campaign. That included a celebrated all-round display against Queensland.

This was Benaud's match. The young Test all-rounder before lunch on the first day, when the pitch was taking some spin, captured five wickets for 17 runs. When New South Wales, facing Queensland's score of 354, had lost four men for 85, Benaud scored 158 of the 264 runs produced in a fifth-wicket stand with Morris. Benaud gave himself time to settle down at the crisis of the innings; later he drove, pulled and hooked with terrific power.

1954–55

AUSTRALIA 1–3 ENGLAND   Norman Preston

Under the zealous and skilful captaincy of Hutton, England won the rubber in Australia for the first time for 22 years and so retained the Ashes they took from Hassett's side at The Oval in 1953. On paper the success gained by the players who sailed from Tilbury in September appears most convincing and rather suggests a comfortable tour against indifferent opposition. That was far from the case. It was a hard tour with its days of triumph and days of regret, but in the end superb fast bowling by Tyson and Statham turned the scales so that finally the Australian batsmen were completely humbled.

Australia v England
First Test Match, at Brisbane, November 26–December 1, 1954
Australia 601-8 dec (R. N. Harvey 162, A. R. Morris 153);
England 190 and 257.
Australia won by an innings and 154 runs.
Benaud: 34; 0-28 and 3-43.

Nothing went right for the Englishmen. Before the match Evans fell ill with sunstroke and on the first morning Compton, when fielding, ran into the wooden palings, breaking a bone in the back of his left hand, but above everything else the whole course of the game probably turned on the decision of Hutton, after winning the toss, to give Australia first innings. Never before had an England captain taken such a gamble in Australia and certainly never before in a Test match had a side replied with a total of 601 after being sent in to bat.

Lindwall and Benaud both hit with great power. Australia, 503 for six at the weekend, kept England in the field until lunchtime on Monday, Lindwall continuing his sparkling hitting which brought him 11 fours. Altogether the Australian innings lasted 11 and a half hours.

Scoring 111 runs in the match Bailey defended resolutely for just under six hours. In less than half an hour after tea the last four wickets fell to the spin of Benaud and Johnson, the match ending with a glorious running catch in the deep by Harvey when Statham tried to lift Benaud for six.

Benaud, opening for the Prime Minister's XI, smashed 113 in 96 minutes against England before the Second Test.

Free hitting was the order of this charity match in which local businessmen offered 30 shillings for each six and ten shillings for each four... They paid out £35 10s, the Englishmen costing them £20... and the Australians £15 10s, five sixes, all by Benaud, and 16 fours... Sir William Slim, the Governor-General of Australia, graced the match with his presence and pleased everyone by "fielding" one of Benaud's sixes in the enclosure.

Australia v England
Second Test Match, at Sydney, December 17–22, 1954
England 154 and **296** (P. B. H. May 104);
Australia 228 and **184** (F. H. Tyson 6-85).
England won by 38 runs.
Benaud: 20 and 12; dnb and 1-42.

Such a victory seemed beyond any possibility when England – this time they were put in by the Australian captain, Morris – lost eight wickets for 88, but among a crop of batting failures in both teams the tailenders made their presence felt. In addition May hit his first Test century against Australia and Neil Harvey made a supreme effort of 92 not out for his side. With ten wickets for 130 runs in the match, Tyson was England's hero.

Australia v England

Third Test Match, at Melbourne, December 31, 1954–January 5, 1955
England 191 (M. C. Cowdrey 102) and **279** (W. A. Johnston 5-85);
Australia 231 (J. B. Statham 5-60) and **111** (F. H. Tyson 7-27).
England won by 128 runs.
Benaud: 15 and 22; 0-30 and 1-25.

As in the previous Test, the combined speed of Tyson and Statham proved too much for Australia and again the two young amateur batsmen, Cowdrey (102) and May (91), carried the England batting on a sporting pitch which was said to have been doctored on the Sunday.

Australia v England

Fourth Test Match, at Adelaide, January 28–February 2, 1955
Australia 323 and **111;**
England 341 and **97-5.**
England won by five wickets.
Benaud: 15 and 1; 4-120 and 0-10.

This victory gave England the rubber for the first time in Australia since 1932-33, and again the fast bowlers, Tyson and Statham, who were well supported by Bailey and Appleyard, played a major part. It was the only match of the series won by the side batting last.

Australia v England

Fifth Test Match, at Sydney, February 25–March 3, 1955
England 371-7 dec (T. W. Graveney 111);
Australia 221 (J. H. Wardle 5-79) and **118-6.**
Drawn.
Benaud: 7 and 22; 1-79.

Abnormal downpours, the worst experienced in New South Wales for 50 years, caused loss of life and millions of pounds of damage in the Hunter River Valley and also held up play in this final Test until 2pm on the fourth day. MCC's tour profits suffered to the extent of nearly £8,000.

At that stage Benaud had a poor Test record, averaging 14 with the bat and 38 with the ball from his first 13 Tests. Things started to change shortly afterwards in the Caribbean.

WEST INDIES 0–3 AUSTRALIA

Following their defeat at home by England, Australia fully rehabilitated themselves in the eyes of the cricket world when visiting the West Indies in 1955. Not only did they complete the tour without a reverse but, in winning three of the Test matches and drawing two, they became the first overseas team to triumph in a series in the Caribbean... Benaud and Archer, both of whom scored maiden Test centuries, accomplished much valuable work as all-rounders.

West Indies v Australia

First Test Match, at Kingston, Jamaica, March 26–31, 1955
Australia 515-9 dec (K. R. Miller 147, R. N. Harvey 133) and **20-1;**
West Indies 259 (C. L. Walcott 108) and **275** (O. G. Smith 104).
Australia won by nine wickets.
Benaud: 46 and dnb; 0-29 and 2-44.

Australia took command from the start. McDonald and Morris began with a partnership of 102 and Harvey, scoring his 13th Test century, and Miller shared in a third-wicket stand of 224. Each hit 15 fours. Profiting from missed chances, Walcott made a brave effort for West Indies, but they could not recover from the loss of five wickets for 101.

West Indies v Australia

Second Test Match, at Port-of-Spain, Trinidad, April 11–16, 1955

West Indies 382 (E. D. Weekes 139, C. L. Walcott 126;

R. R. Lindwall 6-95) and **273-4** (C. L. Walcott 110);

Australia 600-9 dec (R. N. Harvey 133, A. R. Morris 111,

C. C. McDonald 110).

Drawn.

Benaud: 5; 3-43 and 0-52.

A century in each innings by Walcott, who became the third West Indies cricketer to achieve this feat in a Test match, and the return to his best form of Weekes enabled West Indies to share the honours in a game of heavy scoring.

West Indies v Australia

Third Test Match, at Georgetown, Guyana, April 26–29, 1955

West Indies 182 and **207** (I. W. G. Johnson 7-44);

Australia 257 and **133-2.**

Australia won by eight wickets.

Benaud: 68 and dnb; 4-15 and 1-43.

Four West Indies alterations did not strengthen the side in the manner expected, and an unchanged Australian team, despite the absence from the attack of the left-handed Bill Johnston, injured, triumphed with well over two days to spare.

Miller began West Indies' troubles on the first day and by lunchtime five men were out for 86. Weekes did his best to stem the tide, but when he left Benaud, with leg-breaks, caused another collapse, taking four wickets in the course of 23 deliveries for 15 runs. Though McDonald and Morris began with a partnership of 71, Australia lost half their wickets in gaining a lead, and for their first-innings advantage of 75 owed much to brisk hitting by Benaud.

West Indies v Australia

Fourth Test Match, at Bridgetown, Barbados, May 14–20, 1955

Australia 668 (K. R. Miller 137, R. R. Lindwall 118) and **249**

(D. S. Atkinson 5-56);

West Indies 510 (D. S. Atkinson 219, C. C. Depeiza 122) and **234-6**.

Drawn.

Benaud: 1 and 5; 3-73 and 1-35.

This match was rendered memorable by a huge partnership by Atkinson and Depeiza during the first West Indies innings. In putting on 347 they established a world record for the seventh wicket, beating the 344 by K. S. Ranjitsinhji and W. Newham for Sussex against Essex at Leyton in 1902.

West Indies v Australia

Fifth Test Match, at Kingston, Jamaica, June 11–17, 1955

Australia won by an innings and 82 runs.

West Indies

J. K. C. Holt c Langley b Miller	4	–	c Langley b Benaud	21
H. A. Furlonge c Benaud b Lindwall	4	–	c sub (A. K. Davidson) b Miller	28
C. L. Walcott c Langley b Miller	155	–	(4) c Langley b Lindwall	110
E. D. Weekes b Benaud	56	–	(9) not out	36
F. M. M. Worrell c Langley b Lindwall	61	–	(7) b Johnson	12
O. G. Smith c Langley b Miller	29	–	c and b Benaud	16
G. S. Sobers not out	35	–	(5) c Favell b Lindwall	64
*D. St E. Atkinson run out	8	–	c Langley b Archer	4
†C. C. Depeiza c Langley b Miller	0	–	(3) b Miller	7
F. M. King b Miller	0	–	c Archer b Johnson	6
D. T. Dewdney b Miller	2	–	lbw b Benaud	0
L-b 2, w 1	3		B 8, l-b 6, w 1	15
(94.2 overs)	357		(117.5 overs)	319

1/5 (2) 2/13 (1) 3/95 (4) 4/204 (5)   1/47 (1) 2/60 (3) 3/65 (2) 4/244 (5)
5/268 (6) 6/327 (3) 7/341 (8)   5/244 (4) 6/268 (6) 7/273 (8)
8/347 (9) 9/347 (10) 10/357 (11)   8/283 (7) 9/289 (10) 10/319 (11)

Lindwall 12–2–64–2; Miller 25.2–3–107–6; Archer 11–1–39–0; Benaud 24–5–75–1; Johnson 22–7–69–0. *Second innings*—Lindwall 19–6–51–2; Miller 19–3–58–2; Archer 27–6–73–1; Johnson 23–10–46–2; Benaud 29.5–10–76–3.

Australia

C. C. McDonald b Worrell	127	*I. W. G. Johnson not out	27
L. E. Favell c Weekes b King	0	B 8, l-b 7, w 9, n-b 1	25
A. R. Morris lbw b Dewdney	7	(8 wkts dec, 245.4 overs)	758
R. N. Harvey c Atkinson b Smith	204		
K. R. Miller c Worrell b Atkinson	109		
R. G. Archer c Depeiaza b Sobers	128	1/0 (2) 2/7 (3) 3/302 (1) 4/373	
R. R. Lindwall c Depeiaza b King	10	(4) 5/593 (5) 6/597 (6) 7/621	
R. Benaud c Worrell b Smith	121	(7) 8/758 (8)	

†G. R. A. Langley and W. A. Johnston did not bat.

Dewdney 24–4–115–1; King 31–1–126–2; Atkinson 55–20–132–1; Smith 52.4–17–145–2; Worrell 45–10–116–1; Sobers 38–12–99–1.

Umpires: P. Burke and T. A. Ewart.

In a game of many records, first and foremost was the performance of Walcott in hitting for the second time during the series two separate centuries in a match, a feat never before accomplished. The Australian total, besides being the biggest ever recorded in a Test match by a team from the Commonwealth, yielded two other records – the scoring of five centuries in an innings and the highest third-wicket stand in history for Australia. It included a dazzling display of forcing batsmanship by Benaud. So mercilessly did Benaud flog a tiring attack that, with two sixes and 15 fours among his figures, he reached 100 in 78 minutes.

Benaud's remains the third-fastest Test hundred of all time by minutes. The number of balls he faced was not officially recorded, but is thought to be around 75.

1955–56

Benaud succeeded Keith Miller as New South Wales captain and led them to another Sheffield Shield. Wisden said he "led the team with a fine sense of aggression". He also led the list of spin bowlers that season with 25 Shield wickets.

1956

In the summer of 1956, Benaud made his first really significant contribution to an Ashes Test – a counter-attacking 97 in victory at Lord's. But it was otherwise another disappointing series; even though the rubber was dominated by spin, Benaud managed only eight wickets at 41.25 in five Tests.

ENGLAND 2–1 AUSTRALIA Norman Preston

The gradual decline in Australia's cricketing strength since the retirement of Sir Donald Bradman at the end of his triumphant tour of England in 1948 was not halted by the team led by Ian Johnson in 1956. Although they lost the rubber by the bare margin of two wins by England (at Leeds and Manchester) against one by themselves (at Lord's) they were more or less outplayed in four of the five Tests and gave a disappointing display against the majority of the counties.

Their confidence was shaken by the wettest of all summers in memory and in batting, bowling and fielding they were inferior to England... Mackay possessed unbounded patience, as he showed in the Lord's Test when he stayed with Benaud in the vital stand of 117 that left England too big a task in the fourth innings. That day Benaud played the highest innings in the Tests for Australia, 97, but his other eight innings brought him only 103 runs and his leg-break bowling, though successful on occasion against ordinary opposition, did not trouble the best batsmen.

England v Australia

First Test Match, at Nottingham, June 7–12, 1956

England 217-8 dec and **188-3 dec;**

Australia 148 and 120-3.

Drawn.

Benaud: 17 and dnb; dnb and 0-41.

Although England declared twice, the loss of 12 hours and 20 minutes during the match through rain made a definite result impossible. From England's point of view the cricket brought much satisfaction in the batting of Richardson, the Worcestershire left-hander, and Cowdrey.

England v Australia

Second Test Match, at Lord's, June 21–26, 1956

Australia 285 and 257;

England 171 (K. R. Miller 5-72) and **186** (K. R. Miller 5-80).

Australia won by 185 runs.

Benaud: 5 and 97; 2-19 and 1-27.

Australia gained their first Test victory in England since 1948 at The Oval. They went in to the match still without a win against a county side, but proved conclusively that their early form could not be taken as a true guide. The team played splendidly together, took a firm grip on the game and never relaxed. There were several splendid individual performances, notably by Miller, Benaud and Langley, but it was really a triumph of teamwork. England, well served in bowling and fielding, twice failed with the bat.

England looked to be recovering [in their first innings] with Cowdrey and May batting well, but the first of three really brilliant catches in the match ended the stand. Cowdrey hit a ball with tremendous power, but Benaud, in the gully, flung up his hands and held on to it with everyone looking towards the boundary. The force of the ball knocked Benaud backwards.

From Monday morning Australia took control. Benaud set about the bowling so wholeheartedly that England's chances soon waned. Mackay made a passive partner for Benaud. Between them they put on 117 for the seventh wicket of which Benaud made 97, including one six and 14 fours. Trying a big hit to complete his century shortly after Trueman took the new ball, Benaud skyed a catch behind the stumps. He batted two hours 23 minutes and was one of the few batsmen in the match willing to attack. His previous-best score against England was only 34.

England v Australia
Third Test Match, at Leeds, July 12–17, 1956
England 325 (P. B. H. May 101);
Australia 143 (J. C. Laker 5-58) and **140** (J. C. Laker 6-55).
England won by an innings and 42 runs.
Benaud: 30 and 1; 3-89.

Fortunate to win the toss, England looked bound for defeat at the end of the first hour when their first three wickets had fallen to Archer for 17 runs, but a century by May, their captain, and a fine innings of 98 by Washbrook brought about a recovery. Later, Laker, with 11 wickets for 113 runs and Lock, seven for 81, exploited a pitch which favoured slow bowling as early as the second day.

England v Australia
Fourth Test Match, at Manchester, July 26–31, 1956
England 459 (Rev D. S. Sheppard 113, P. E. Richardson 104);
Australia 84 (J. C. Laker 9-37) and **205** (J. C. Laker 10-53).
England won by an innings and 170 runs.
Benaud: 0 and 18; 2-123.

England won by an innings and 170 runs with just over an hour to spare and so retained the Ashes. This memorable game will always be known as Laker's Match because of the remarkable performance by the Surrey off-break bowler in taking nine wickets for 37 runs in the first innings, and ten wickets for 53 in the second. Laker broke all the important bowling records in the history of cricket. Johnson and Benaud, the Australian spin bowlers, were unable to exploit the conditions.

Benaud had more success in the tour game at Edgbaston, taking five for 44 and six for 31 in an innings victory over Warwickshire.

Warwickshire gave a disappointing display, twice collapsing on a pitch that offered little help to the bowlers. They never mastered Benaud, who accomplished his best work of the tour with the ball in taking 11 wickets for 75 runs... After Burke caught Spooner off his bowling Benaud got Smith taken at first slip next ball and only narrowly missed a hat-trick, for Stewart knew little about the following ball that just passed the off stump.

England v Australia

Fifth Test Match, at The Oval, August 23–28, 1956

England 247 (R. G. Archer 5-53) and **182-3 dec;**

Australia 202 and **27-5.**

Drawn.

Benaud: 32 and 0*; 0-21 and 0-10.

Australia needed to win this match to save the rubber – the Ashes already belonged to England – but with 12 hours and 20 minutes of the 30 hours allocated to the game lost through rain, a definite result could not be reached. In any case, England generally dominated the struggle, and Australia, who in both of their innings lost half their wickets for less than 50, were fighting a rearguard action after tea on the last day.

When England began their second innings on a drying pitch one had visions of Australia taking complete revenge for their collapses in the two previous Tests. Every time the ball pitched it left its mark. Laker and Lock would have been almost unplayable, but Australia possessed no spin bowler capable of taking advantage of the conditions.

After shredding Scotland with six for 34 in an end-of-tour game, Benaud demonstrated the gift for public relations that would serve him so well when he later became captain.

The Australian spin bowlers achieved considerable success, notably Benaud. When the match was over the Australians gave a batting exhibition for an hour during which Burge and Benaud pleased the crowd by hitting a number of sixes.

1956–57

After taking no five-wicket hauls in his first 24 Tests, Benaud claimed three in as many matches on his first Test tour of the subcontinent, including figures of 11 for 105 that would remain his career-best.

PAKISTAN 1–0 AUSTRALIA

Pakistan v Australia
Only Test Match, at Karachi, October 11–17, 1956
Australia 80 (Fazal Mahmood 6-34) and **187** (Fazal Mahmood 7-80);
Pakistan 199 and **69-1.**
Pakistan won by nine wickets.
Benaud: 4 and 56; 1-36 and dnb.

By this emphatic success the youngest member of the Imperial Cricket Conference confirmed the excellent impression formed two years previously when they defeated England at The Oval. Perhaps the Australians, travel weary, suffered some reaction as the result of their strenuous tour of England, and the immediate change from grass to matting without any prolonged practice in the altered conditions could not have been easy for them.

INDIA 0–2 AUSTRALIA

India v Australia
First Test Match, at Madras (now Chennai), October 19–23, 1956
India 161 (R. Benaud 7-72) and **153** (R. R. Lindwall 7-43);
Australia 319.
Australia won by an innings and 5 runs.
Benaud: 6; 7-72 and 1-59.

The Australians found the turf pitch much more to their liking than the matting at Karachi, and comfortably won the first Test to be played between the two countries in India. Excessive caution on the opening day had much to do with India's downfall. Australia were sorely handicapped by mishaps to their pace bowlers. Miller, Archer and Davidson could not play because of injuries, and Lindwall retired with a stomach complaint after bowling five overs. Yet India scored only 117 for five in a full day, Crawford, the one remaining bowler of pace, and Benaud with leg-breaks rising to the occasion well. Benaud caused the last five wickets to tumble for 44 on the second day.

India v Australia

Second Test Match, at Bombay (now Mumbai), October 26–31, 1956
India 251 (G. S. Ramchand 109) and **250-5;**
Australia 523-7 dec (J. W. Burke 161, R. N. Harvey 140).
Drawn.
Benaud: 2; 2-54 and 2-98.

Conditions favoured Australia throughout the five days. Their pace attack gained considerable assistance from the pitch in India's first innings, and had Crawford not been forced to leave the field with a muscular injury after taking three wickets for 28 on the first day, the total might have been considerably less. Australia, in turn, batted on an easy surface, and India's bowling came in for merciless treatment by Burke and Harvey. The pitch had deteriorated by the time India batted again, and every ball from Benaud, Davidson and Wilson kicked up a puff of dust, the result of overnight covering of the entire pitch.

India v Australia

Third Test Match, at Calcutta (now Kolkata), November 2–6, 1956

Australia won by 94 runs.

Australia

C. C. McDonald b Ghulam Ahmed	3	– lbw b Ramchand	0
J. W. Burke c Manjrekar b Ghulam Ahmed	10	– c Contractor b Ghulam Ahmed	2
R. N. Harvey c Tamhane b Ghulam Ahmed	7	– c Umrigar b Mankad	69
I. D. Craig c Tamhane b Gupte	36	– b Ghulam Ahmed	6
P. J. P. Burge c Ramchand b Ghulam Ahmed	58	– c Ramchand b Ghulam Ahmed	22
K. D. Mackay lbw b Mankad	5	– hit wkt b Mankad	27
R. Benaud b Ghulam Ahmed	24	– b Gupte	21
R. R. Lindwall b Ghulam Ahmed	8	– c Tamhane b Mankad	28
*I. W. G. Johnson c Ghulam Ahmed b Mankad	1	– st Tamhane b Mankad	5
W. P. A. Crawford c Contractor b Ghulam Ahmed	18	– not out	1
†G. R. A. Langley not out	1		
B 6	6	B 6, l-b 2	8
(86.3 overs)	177	(9 wkts dec, 67.4 overs)	189

1/6 (1) 2/22 (3) 3/25 (2) 4/93 (4)
5/106 (6) 6/141 (5) 7/152 (7) 8/157 (8)
9/163 (9) 10/177 (10)

1/0 (1) 2/9 (2) 3/27 (4) 4/59 (5)
5/122 (6) 6/149 (7) 7/159 (3)
8/188 (8) 9/189 (9)

Ramchand 2–1–1–0; Umrigar 16–3–30–0; Ghulam Ahmed 20.3–6–49–7; Gupte 23–11–35–1; Mankad 25–4–56–2. *Second innings*—Ramchand 2–1–6–1; Umrigar 20–9–21–0; Ghulam Ahmed 29–5–81–3; Mankad 9.4–1–49–4; Gupte 7–1–24–1.

India

Pankaj Roy b Lindwall	13	– lbw b Burke	24
N. J. Contractor lbw b Benaud	22	– b Johnson	20
*P. R. Umrigar c Burge b Johnson	5	– c Burke b Benaud	28
V. L. Manjrekar c Harvey b Benaud	33	– c Harvey b Benaud	22
V. Mankad lbw b Benaud	4	– c Harvey b Benaud	24
G. S. Ramchand st Langley b Benaud	2	– b Burke	3
A. G. Kripal Singh c Mackay b Benaud	14	– b Benaud	0
P. Bhandari lbw b Lindwall	17	– c Harvey b Burke	2
†N. S. Tamhane b Benaud	5	– b Benaud	0
Ghulam Ahmed c Mackay b Lindwall	10	– b Burke	0
S. P. Gupte not out	1	– not out	0
B 7, l-b 1, n-b 2	10	B 5, l-b 5, n-b 3	13
(78.2 overs)	136	(69.2 overs)	136

1/15 (1) 2/20 (3) 3/76 (2) 4/80 (5)
5/82 (6) 6/98 (7) 7/99 (4) 8/115 (9)
9/135 (8) 10/136 (10)

1/44 (2) 2/50 (1) 3/94 (4) 4/99 (3)
5/102 (6) 6/121 (7) 7/134 (5)
8/136 (8) 9/136 (10) 10/136 (9)

Lindwall 25.2–12–32–3; Crawford 3–3–0–0; Johnson 12–2–27–1; Benaud 29–10–52–6; Harvey 1–1–0–0; Burke 8–3–15–0. *Second innings*—Lindwall 12–7–9–0; Crawford 2–1–1–0; Benaud 24.2–6–53–5; Johnson 14–5–23–1; Burke 17–4–37–4.

Umpires: G. Ayling and B. J. Mohoni.

The pitch took spin from the start, and 35 of the 39 wickets fell to slow bowlers. Umrigar, sending in Australia, wasted little time in bringing on Ghulam Ahmed. The off-spinner took three wickets for three runs in 6.2 overs before he missed a return catch from Craig, who with Burge added 68 runs for the fourth wicket. Altogether, Ghulam took seven wickets for 49 runs and India, having dismissed Australia for 177, seemed favourably placed. Rain overnight delayed the resumption by 65 minutes but all went well before the turf dried. Then the leg-breaks of Benaud began to bite, and India were 41 runs behind when their first innings closed. Mankad joined with Ghulam in worrying Australia in their second innings, but valuable batting for three hours by Harvey plus bold hitting by the later batsmen meant that India required 231 runs to win. As in their first innings, India scored steadily until lunch, when the total was 74 for two. Then Benaud, helped by Burke with off-breaks, brought a speedy end to the game, the last five wickets falling while 15 runs were scored. Benaud gained match figures of 11 wickets for 105 runs.

Four years before the first Tied Test, Benaud was involved in the first tied Sheffield Shield match, between New South Wales and Victoria.

Craig, suffering from tonsillitis, and Burke, with a broken finger, batted for New South Wales in their second innings and helped in the first tie in the 100 years' history of inter-State cricket. On a drying pitch New South Wales needed 161 runs for victory. When seven wickets fell for 70 they seemed sure to be beaten, but Craig and Benaud shared a stand of 75 for the eighth wicket.

In February 1957, a strong Australian side toured New Zealand. Benaud struck two centuries, against Poverty Bay and Central Districts, and took six for 79 in an unofficial Test.

Undoubtedly Australia's best player was Benaud. He batted forcibly; took most wickets with his leg-breaks and in fielding, too, he stood out in a side which, becoming youth, displayed very good outcricket.

1957–58

This was the tour that changed Benaud's career. He produced a stream of exceptional all-round performances, taking a short cut to the cusp of greatness.

SOUTH AFRICA 0–3 AUSTRALIA

The Australians restored their sagging prestige with a highly successful tour of South Africa and their splendid form raised their hopes that they would recover the Ashes when England toured their country a year later.

The outstanding personality was Benaud, who, in bowling and batting, enjoyed a tour of unbroken success. Adding the googly to his leg-break and top-spinner, Benaud once more revealed the South Africans' dislike of flighted spin, bowled out of the back of the hand. The previous year Wardle, of similar type, but left-handed, took 90 wickets in first-class matches on the tour; Benaud did even better with 106, two more than any other bowler on a tour of South Africa. Thirty of his wickets came in the Test matches, and four times he took five wickets in an innings against South

Africa. Only in the First Test did Benaud fail to cause chaos with the ball, but he scored 122 in that match. He also hit another century in the Fourth Test. Benaud's aggressive batting made him a great favourite with the crowds, and his all-round skill was a major factor in the Australian success.

In the opening match of the tour, against Northern Rhodesia, Benaud returned staggering first-innings figures of 10–4–16–9. A week later he made 117 not out against Rhodesia, adding an unbroken 177 for the seventh wicket with Alan Davidson, and then claimed six for 95 in the second innings. Soon after came seven for 46 against Natal, career-best figures at the time, and 13 for 134 in the match, and then a ten-for against Eastern Province. All that, and the Test series had not even started.

South Africa v Australia
First Test Match, at Johannesburg, December 23–28, 1957
South Africa 470-9 dec (J. H. B. Waite 115, D. J. McGlew 108;
I. Meckiff 5-125) and **201** (A. K. Davidson 6-34);
Australia 368 (R. Benaud 122; P. S. Heine 6-58) and **162-3.**
Drawn.
Benaud: 122 and dnb; 1-115 and 0-15.

A thoroughly entertaining match ended with honours even, although for the most part Australia had to fight an uphill battle. Benaud and Simpson, in his first Test, led the recovery. Benaud, batting splendidly, completed his century on the third morning and did most to restrict South Africa's lead to 102.

South Africa v Australia
Second Test Match, at Cape Town, December 31, 1957–January 3, 1958
Australia 449 (J. W. Burke 189; H. J. Tayfield 5-120);
South Africa 209 and **99** (R. Benaud 5-49).
Australia won by an innings and 141 runs.
Benaud: 33; 4-95 and 5-49.

Australia thoroughly outplayed South Africa, making the most of the big advantage gained in winning the toss. The match ended dramatically with a hat-trick by Kline, the left-arm googly bowler. Spin was more effective than speed, and Benaud and Kline caused the collapse. Benaud made good use of top-spin and Kline exploited the googly successfully.

The match ended soon after lunch on the fourth day when eight wickets fell for 32. Benaud again caused most trouble until Kline brought a hasty finish by dismissing Fuller, Tayfield and Adcock with successive balls.

Benaud continued on his merry way against Natal, striking a career-best 187 a week before the Third Test.

South Africa v Australia
Third Test Match, at Durban, January 24–29, 1958
Australia 163 (N. A. T. Adcock 6-43) and **292-7;**
South Africa 384 (J. H. B. Waite 134, D. J. McGlew 105; R. Benaud 5-114).
Drawn.
Benaud: 12 and 4; 5-114.

South Africa went close to recording the first victory in their own country against Australia, but although undoubtedly the better side in the match they contributed towards their own failure to win by surprising and unnecessarily slow batting. The pitch eased a good deal, but subsequently took spin, and Benaud played the leading part while the last five wickets fell in 100 minutes on the fourth morning for 66.

South Africa v Australia

Fourth Test Match, at Johannesburg, February 7–12, 1958

Australia won by ten wickets.

Australia

C. C. McDonald lbw b Tayfield	26	– not out	1
J. W. Burke c Waite b Heine	81	– not out	0
R. N. Harvey c Waite b Goddard	5		
R. Benaud c Endean b Heine	100		
*I. D. Craig b Heine	3		
†A. T. W. Grout lbw b Adcock	7		
K. D. Mackay not out	83		
R. B. Simpson c Waite b Adcock	6		
A. K. Davidson c Burger b Heine	62		
I. Meckiff c Endean b Heine	26		
L. F. Kline c Waite b Heine	1		
L-b 1	1		—
(149.5 overs)	**401**	**(no wkt, 0.4 overs)**	**1**

1/43 (1) 2/52 (3) 3/210 (4) 4/213 (5)
5/222 (2) 6/222 (6) 7/234 (8) 8/315 (9)
9/393 (10) 10/401 (11)

Heine 37.5–6–96–6; Adcock 17–3–37–2; Goddard 43–10–136–1; Tayfield 49–17–107–1; van Ryneveld 3–0–24–0. *Second innings*—McLean 0.4–0–1–0.

South Africa

D. J. McGlew c Grout b Meckiff	1	– c Simpson b Benaud	70
W. R. Endean lbw b Davidson	22	– c Simpson b Benaud	38
H. J. Tayfield lbw b Benaud	27	– (9) st Grout b Kline	0
T. L. Goddard c and b Meckiff	9	– (3) c Simpson b Benaud	0
K. J. Funston c Craig b Kline	70	– (4) not out	64
R. A. McLean c Grout b Davidson	9	– (5) c Grout b Davidson	0
C. G. D. Burger st Grout b Kline	21	– c McDonald b Kline	1
†J. H. B. Waite lbw b Benaud	12	– (6) c Grout b Benaud	10
P. S. Heine c and b Benaud	24	– (10) c Meckiff b Benaud	1
N. A. T. Adcock b Benaud	0	– (11) run out	3
*C. B. van Ryneveld not out	0	– (8) lbw b Kline	0
B 3, w 2, n-b 3	8	L-b 8, w 2, n-b 1	11
(80.2 overs)	**203**	**(105 overs)**	**198**

1/17 (1) 2/27 (2) 3/46 (4) 4/104 (3)   1/78 (2) 2/78 (3) 3/147 (1) 4/148 (5)
5/115 (6) 6/166 (5) 7/166 (7) 8/186 (8)   5/161 (6) 6/180 (7) 7/180 (8) 8/182 (9)
9/194 (10) 10/203 (9)   9/183 (10) 10/198 (11)

Meckiff 21–3–38–2; Davidson 19–2–39–2; Mackay 11–5–11–0; Benaud 20.2–0–70–4; Kline 9–1–37–2. *Second innings*—Meckiff 13–2–24–0; Davidson 20–4–44–1; Benaud 41–8–84–5; Burke 15–10–8–0; Kline 16–6–27–3.

Umpires: A. Birkett and J. H. McMenamin.

Australia won by ten wickets and made certain of the rubber. Once again South Africa's batting disappointed on an easy pitch and only by a single run did they avoid an innings defeat.

Craig made a wise move in promoting Benaud to No. 4, and he and Burke thoroughly mastered the attack. South Africa were handicapped after lunch when Adcock retired with influenza and Heine reduced his pace because of ankle trouble. Benaud, after playing himself in, attacked the bowling and completed an excellent century before he skyed a hook.

South Africa v Australia

Fifth Test Match, at Port Elizabeth, February 28–March 4, 1958

South Africa 214 and **144** (A. K. Davidson 5-38, R. Benaud 5-82);

Australia 291 and **68-2.**

Australia won by eight wickets.

Benaud: 43 and 6*; 1-34 and 5-82.

Australia won by eight wickets with a day to spare and completed a great Test series on their part. Once again the South African batting failed and the game provided yet another triumph for Benaud and Davidson. Benaud took his 100th Test wicket and completed the double of 1,000 runs and 100 wickets. He also achieved the rare feat of taking 100 wickets on a tour.

Benaud ended the five-Test series with 329 runs at 54.83 and 30 wickets at 21.93. Including tour matches, he made 817 runs at 51.06 and claimed 106 wickets at 19.39. The following winter, he was a marginal choice ahead of the more experienced Neil Harvey to replace the indisposed Ian Craig as Australian captain. His side were given little chance against an England team which had not lost a series for eight years. It turned out to be one of the greatest shocks in Test history.

1958–59

AUSTRALIA 4–0 ENGLAND

Australia, under Benaud, their new captain, won the 1958-59 Test series against the visiting England team, led by May, so convincingly that English enthusiasts were left wondering how their favourites came to lose the Ashes which they had held since 1953.

England certainly had a number of injuries, but neither this factor nor complaints about umpiring and the doubtful actions of several bowlers could gainsay the fact that the tourists were not good enough. This was the basic reason for their disappointing displays against an Australian side which, though excellent as a team, was far from brilliant in individual achievement.

Australia possessed an inspiring leader in Benaud. He set an example of keen and fearless fielding by often posting himself close to the bat and, except for the Third Test when, with Australia two victories to the good, he closed up the game with an exaggerated defensive field, his handling of the team did him credit. Moreover, his bowling prowess with the leg-break, top-spinner and googly made him one of Australia's best players.

May, as a player – probably the finest batsman in the world – ranked as high as his rival, but there the comparison ended. May never seemed to communicate to his team the driving force which Benaud gave to Australia.

May's field-settings were stereotyped, especially in the placings for his fast bowlers with the new ball. Benaud, in contrast, backed up the efforts of Davidson, Meckiff, Ray Lindwall and Gordon Rorke with the most intimidating fields he could devise.

Benaud prepared for the Ashes by routing Western Australia with 11 wickets in the match and a dashing 76.

Australia v England
First Test Match, at Brisbane, December 5–10, 1958
England 134 and 198;
Australia 186 and 147-2.
Australia won by eight wickets.
Benaud: 16 and dnb; 3-46 and 4-66.

England, contrary to expectations, were beaten. The turning point came on the fourth day when Graveney was run out and Cowdrey given out caught by Kline though many present were convinced that a catch had not been made. England, who had been gaining a grip on the game after a breakdown in the first innings, lost their hold and surrendered the initiative to Australia, who were inspiringly led by Benaud, the new captain.

Between the First and Second Tests Benaud returned to New South Wales, and ran through Victoria over Christmas.

Benaud set Victoria to make 301 runs in 283 minutes, but the last seven wickets fell for 11 runs. Benaud took six wickets for six runs in 39 deliveries at one stage.

Australia v England
Second Test Match, at Melbourne, December 31, 1958–January 5, 1959
England 259 (P. B. H. May 113; A. K. Davidson 6-64) and **87** (I. Meckiff 6-38);
Australia 308 (R. N. Harvey 167; J. B. Statham 7-57) and **42-2.**
Australia won by eight wickets.
Benaud: 0 and dnb; 1-61 and 0-4.

England were set back on their heels from the start when Davidson took three wickets in a sensational over, and although Statham also bowled finely the tourists never really recovered.

The match produced a hostile bowling effort by the left-arm Meckiff, whose jerky action brought much criticism. The pitch, faster than at Brisbane, allowed batsmen to make strokes and also enabled the quick bowlers to show their paces. Australia nearly always held the mastery. Harvey excelled in a fine innings of 167 for the winners, who brilliantly accepted their catching chances.

Australia v England

Third Test Match, at Sydney, January 9–15, 1959

England 219 (R. Benaud 5-83) and **287-7 dec** (M. C. Cowdrey 100*);

Australia 357 (J. C. Laker 5-107) and **54-2.**

Drawn.

Benaud: 6 and dnb; 5-83 and 4-94.

England, knowing that defeat would mean the loss of the Ashes, fought with more spirit after another first-innings breakdown had put them in serious danger, and emerged with an honourable draw. Benaud bowled well in taking nine wickets for 177 runs.

The second-day crowd saw England out in 50 minutes, the last three wickets falling to Benaud, who turned the ball appreciably, in nine deliveries for eight runs. In this deadly spell magnificent one-handed catches by Mackay at forward short leg and Harvey at slip helped in England's downfall. Harvey's was a really wonderful effort.

England, 40 ahead with seven wickets in hand, were reasonably well placed for the last day. May's strategy was to go for runs hoping that they would come quickly enough to permit a declaration and provide his spinners with the chance to try to bring off a long-shot victory. Benaud, in retaliation, once again set a defensive field even for the new ball taken by Davidson and Slater.

Benaud also took a five-for against MCC in a tour match for New South Wales, all of which came during a spell of 5.2–1–11–5

Australia v England

Fourth Test Match, at Adelaide, January 30–February 5, 1959

Australia won by ten wickets.

Australia

C. C. McDonald b Trueman	170			
J. W. Burke c Cowdrey b Bailey	66	– not out		16
R. N. Harvey run out	41			
N. C. O'Neill b Statham	56			
L. E. Favell b Statham	4	– (1) not out		15
K. D. Mackay c Evans b Statham	4			
*R. Benaud b Trueman	46			
A. K. Davidson c Bailey b Tyson	43			
†A. T. W. Grout lbw b Trueman	9			
R. R. Lindwall b Trueman	19			
G. F. Rorke not out	2			
B 2, l-b 8, w 4, n-b 2	16	B 4, l-b 1		5
(128.1 overs)	476	(no wkt, 10.3 overs)		36

1/171 (2) 2/276 (3) 3/286 (5) 4/294 (6)
5/369 (4) 6/388 (7) 7/407 (9) 8/445 (8)
9/473 (1) 10/476 (10)

Statham 23–0–83–3; Trueman 30.1–6–90–4; Tyson 28–1–100–1; Bailey 22–2–91–1; Lock 25–0–96–0. *Second innings*—Statham 4–0–11–0; Trueman 3–1–3–0; Lock 2–0–8–0; Cowdrey 1.3–0–9–0.

England

P. E. Richardson lbw b Lindwall	4	– lbw b Benaud		43
T. E. Bailey b Davidson	4	– (6) c Grout b Lindwall		6
*P. B. H. May b Benaud	37	– lbw b Rorke		59
M. C. Cowdrey b Rorke	84	– b Lindwall		8
T. W. Graveney c Benaud b Rorke	41	– not out		53
W. Watson b Rorke	25	– (2) c Favell b Benaud		40
F. S. Trueman c Grout b Benaud	0	– c Grout b Davidson		0
G. A. R. Lock c Grout b Benaud	2	– b Rorke		9
F. H. Tyson c and b Benaud	0	– c Grout b Benaud		33
†T. G. Evans c Burke b Benaud	4	– (11) c Benaud b Davidson		0
J. B. Statham not out	36	– (10) c O'Neill b Benaud		2
L-b 2, n-b 1	3	B 5, l-b 5, w 3, n-b 4		17
(74.1 overs)	240	(101.3 overs)		270

1/7 (1) 2/11 (2) 3/74 (3) 4/170 (4)   1/89 (2) 2/110 (1) 3/125 (4) 4/177 (3)
5/173 (5) 6/180 (7) 7/184 (8) 8/184 (9)   5/198 (6) 6/199 (7) 7/222 (8) 8/268 (9)
9/188 (10) 10/240 (6)   9/270 (10) 10/270 (11)

Davidson 12–0–49–1; Lindwall 15–0–66–1; Rorke 18.1–7–23–3; Benaud 27–6–91–5; O'Neill 2–1–8–0. *Second innings*—Lindwall 26–6–70–2; Rorke 34–7–78–2; Benaud 29–10–82–4; Davidson 8.3–3–17–2; Burke 4–2–6–0.

Umpires: M. J. McInnes and R. J. J. Wright.

Australia won by ten wickets and regained the Ashes. Their success was well deserved, being even more decisive than those at Brisbane and Melbourne. May, knowing that he had to win as a draw was useless for the retention of the Ashes, took the bold course of sending Australia in to bat, but his hopes were not realised. McDonald proved Australia's match-winning batsman and Benaud, besides inspiring his colleagues by splendid fielding, displayed his capabilities as a dangerous bowler.

Australia v England
Fifth Test Match, at Melbourne, February 13–18, 1959
England 205 and 214;
Australia 351 (C. C. McDonald 133) and **69-1.**
Australia won by nine wickets.
Benaud: 64 and dnb; 4-43 and 1-14.

England virtually lost before play began, for a car accident in which Loader and Statham were hurt ruled these two out of consideration. Benaud, with four fast bowlers given him by the Australian selectors, put England in and his policy was fully justified – the first occasion victory had attended a captain who put his rivals in since J. W. H. T. Douglas did so in 1911-12.

The England fast attack suffered severe punishment at the hands of Benaud and Grout, who used the hook as his main scoring stroke, in a lively stand of two and a quarter hours. Trueman sent back Lindwall and Meckiff in one over, but Benaud, with Rorke last man in, monopolised the strike and Australia reached 351 before their captain skyed a catch which Swetman took at short square leg.

1959–60

After regaining the Ashes from England the previous winter, the Australians completed a short but highly successful tour of the subcontinent in 1959-60. Of the bowlers, Benaud was the most successful with his leg-spin, accounting altogether for 49 victims, 47 of them in the Tests. He outshone the battery of fast bowlers who had been expected to do so much.

PAKISTAN 0–2 AUSTRALIA

Pakistan v Australia

First Test Match, at Dacca (now Dhaka), November 13–18, 1959

Pakistan 200 and **134** (K. D. Mackay 6-42);

Australia 225 (Fazal Mahmood 5-71) and **112-2**.

Australia won by eight wickets.

Benaud: 16 and dnb; 4-69 and 4-42.

Heavy rain prior to the match ruled out the possibility of it being played on grass and Pakistan, sent in by Benaud, were all out for 200. Australia, too, found scoring difficult and despite an excellent innings of 96 by Harvey, they only secured a first-innings lead through Grout, whose spirited 66 not out, including seven fours, came in an hour and 25 minutes. Mackay, bowling off-spinners on a perfect length, severely troubled Pakistan when they batted a second time and he finished with six for 42.

Pakistan v Australia

Second Test Match, at Lahore, November 21–26, 1959

Pakistan 146 and **366** (Saeed Ahmed 166; L. F. Kline 7-75);

Australia 391-9 dec (N. C. O'Neill 134) and **123-3**.

Australia won by seven wickets.

Benaud 29 and 21*; 2-36 and 2-92.

Australia won by seven wickets and clinched the series, becoming the first country to win a Test rubber in Pakistan. Pakistan always struggled during their first innings against the pace of Davidson and Meckiff, and the spin of Benaud and Kline, despite the easy nature of the turf pitch. When the last day began, Pakistan stood 43 ahead with seven wickets in hand, but Kline, with his left-arm slows, exploited worn patches and brought about a collapse. Australia needed 122 in just under two hours and achieved victory with 12 minutes to spare, Harvey, O'Neill and Benaud all batting confidently.

Pakistan v Australia

Third Test Match, at Karachi, December 4–9, 1959

Pakistan 287 (R. Benaud 5-93) and **194-8 dec**

(Hanif Mohammad 101*);

Australia 257 (Fazal Mahmood 5-74) and **83-2;**

Drawn.

Benaud: 18 and dnb; 5-93 and 1-48.

With Australia two wins ahead in the series and Pakistan beaten at home for the first time in a rubber, there seemed every chance of some lively cricket. In fact, play was drab for most of the time, with Pakistan taking eight hours 48 minutes over 287 in their first innings and eight hours over 194 in their second. Mr Eisenhower watched play on the fourth day and, as he was the first United States President to see Test cricket, his visit may well be remembered long after this disappointing game is forgotten.

INDIA 1–2 AUSTRALIA

India v Australia

First Test Match, at Delhi, December 12–16, 1959

India 135 and **206** (R. Benaud 5-76);

Australia 468 (R. N. Harvey 114).

Australia won by an innings and 127 runs.

Benaud: 20; 3-0 and 5-76.

Splendid spin bowling by their captain, Benaud, and fast scoring by Harvey and the tailenders, Grout and Meckiff, were chiefly responsible for Australia's winning with just over a day to spare. Benaud gained the unusual figures of three wickets for no runs in India's first innings, and with Kline, the left-arm spin bowler, dismissed them cheaply when they batted again 334 behind. Roy and Contractor gave India a good start when they replied, scoring 121 before being separated, but Benaud and Kline hustled the next nine batsmen out for the addition of 85 runs, and at the end disappointed spectators threw bottles on the field as India crumbled to an ignominious defeat.

India v Australia

Second Test Match, at Kanpur, December 19–24, 1959

India 152 (A. K. Davidson 5-31) and **291** (A. K. Davidson 7-93);

Australia 219 (J. M. Patel 9-69) and **105** (J. M. Patel 5-55).

India won by 119 runs.

Benaud: 7 and 0; 4-63 and 1-81.

The chief architect of India's first Test victory over Australia since the two countries first met in 1947 was Patel, the Ahmedabad off-spin bowler, who took 14 wickets for 124 runs. In the Australian first innings Patel exploited newly laid turf and achieved an analysis of nine for 69 – India's finest Test bowling performance. Then on the last day, amid scenes of great excitement, he routed Australia a second time and took five more wickets for 55 runs.

India v Australia

Third Test Match, at Bombay, January 1–6, 1960

India 289 (N. J. Contractor 108) and **226-5 dec;**

Australia 387-8 dec (N. C. O'Neill 163, R. N. Harvey 102;

R. G. Nadkarni 6-105) and **34-1.**

Drawn.

Benaud: 14 and 12*; 1-64 and 0-36.

India suffered a blow when Patel, their match-winning bowler of the Second Test, reported sick on the morning of the match. A determined opening partnership by Roy and Contractor, and more sound batting by Baig and Kenny, made India safe, and when they declared Australia had only 25 minutes in which to make 129 – an impossible task.

India v Australia

Fourth Test Match, at Madras (now Chennai), January 13–17, 1960

Australia 342 (L. E. Favell 101);

India 149 (R. Benaud 5-43) and **138.**

Australia won by an innings and 55 runs.

Benaud: 25; 5-43 and 3-43.

A fine spell by Benaud, who turned his leg-breaks appreciably and dismissed four batsmen for seven runs, wrecked India's hopes. Only the wicketkeeper, Kunderan, appeared confident and his 71 included 12 fours. Following on 193 runs behind, India batted feebly. Again Benaud was mainly responsible for their failure. He captured three key wickets for 43 runs and finished with a match analysis of eight wickets for 86. He repeatedly changed the bowling, allowing the batsmen little opportunity to settle down.

India v Australia

Fifth Test Match, at Calcutta (now Kolkata), January 23–28, 1960

India 194 and 339;

Australia 331 (N. C. O'Neill 113) and **121-2.**

Drawn.

Benaud 3 and 10*; 3-59 and 4-103.

India needed to win to share the rubber and their hopes shattered on the first day when they lost half their side for 112. Careful batting by Gopinath and Jaisimha improved the situation, but early on the second morning Davidson virtually finished the innings by removing Ramchand and Desai.

India, needing 137 to avoid an innings defeat, began their second innings badly, losing Kunderan for a duck. The position deteriorated to 123 for five before a stand of 83 between Jaisimha and Borde effected a partial recovery. Both scored well, Borde being especially severe on Benaud with powerful cuts and drives.

Upon returning to Australia, Benaud helped New South Wales set a new record by winning a seventh consecutive Sheffield Shield. In his only match of the season, he captained the side against Western Australia and took six for 74 in each innings to secure the title in a race against a thunderstorm.

1960–61

In Wisden 1961, *Norman Preston hailed Benaud in his Editor's Notes.*

As this depressing year was reaching its close Australia and West Indies lit the torch to the path of brighter cricket by playing a tie at the Woolloongabba ground, Brisbane. It was the first tie in the long history of 500 Test matches and there was scarcely a dull moment throughout the five days... How was the miracle achieved in this age of so much unimaginative and negative cricket? It was achieved by Richie Benaud and Frank Worrell, the rival captains. First of all they were blessed with ideal conditions, sunshine and a perfect pitch, two important factors. Just as important was the attitude of both men to the game. These captains insisted that the men under their command played enterprising cricket from the very first ball, and they did not think of withdrawing into their shells when they ran into trouble. They still put victory as their goal and the stories of their deeds right through the series thrilled the cricket world.

Many people are anxious about the future of the first-class game. One cannot control the weather, but when it is favourable the destiny of cricket is in the hands of the captains. Benaud and Worrell have proved this truism. You can vary the Laws and do what you like, but without the goodwill of the captains all is in vain.

AUSTRALIA 2–1 WEST INDIES

Never has it been more apparent that the game is greater than the result than in Melbourne on February 17, 1961. Commerce in this Australian city stood almost still as the smiling cricketers from the West Indies, the vanquished not the victors, were given a send-off the like of which is normally reserved for royalty and national heroes. Open cars paraded the happy players from the Caribbean among hundreds of thousands of Australians who had been senti-mentalised through the medium of cricket as it should be played.

Four months earlier these same players had arrived almost unsung but vowing, through their captain Frank Worrell, that they were going to re-instil some lost adventure into cricket, which for several years had in the main been a dull, lifeless pastime to watch internationally.

The forthright Australian captain, Richie Benaud, supported him. Cynics, and the not-so-cynical, who had witnessed so much drab play over the last decade or so, thought they had heard it all before. Too much was at stake nationally, they argued, for any lightness of heart to prevail.

Worrell and Benaud and their associates happily proved them wrong. Summer's glorious pastime had returned as a spectacle of some consequence and faith in the game was restored among the all-important younger fraternity on whom its popularity, and indeed its very existence, depends.

That Worrell and Benaud were the leaders cannot be stressed too much. Upon their insistence on attractive, sensible cricket was laid the foundations of a true demon-stration of this great game.

Benaud took 23 wickets but it was perhaps his lead-ership rather than his bowling which brought most commendation on this occasion. Proof that he was deter-mined to play the game the right way until the very end came when he won the toss in the final Test and put West Indies in to bat – a courageous decision at such a vital stage.

Australia v West Indies

First Test Match, at Brisbane, December 9–14, 1960

Tied.

West Indies

C. C. Hunte c Benaud b Davidson	24	– c Simpson b Mackay	39
C. W. Smith c Grout b Davidson	7	– c O'Neill b Davidson	6
R. B. Kanhai c Grout b Davidson	15	– c Grout b Davidson	54
G. S. Sobers c Kline b Meckiff	132	– b Davidson	14
*F. M. M. Worrell c Grout b Davidson	65	– c Grout b Davidson	65
J. S. Solomon hit wkt b Simpson	65	– lbw b Simpson	47
P. D. Lashley c Grout b Kline	19	– b Davidson	0
†F. C. M. Alexander c Davidson b Kline	60	– b Benaud	5
S. Ramadhin c Harvey b Davidson	12	– c Harvey b Simpson	6
W. W. Hall st Grout b Kline	50	– b Davidson	18
A. L. Valentine not out	0	– not out	7
L-b 3, w 1	4	B 14, l-b 7, w 2	23
(100.6 overs)	453	(92.6 overs)	284

1/23 (2) 2/42 (1) 3/65 (3) 4/239 (4)
5/243 (5) 6/283 (7) 7/347 (6) 8/366 (9)
9/452 (10) 10/453 (8)

1/13 (2) 2/88 (1) 3/114 (4) 4/127 (3)
5/210 (5) 6/210 (7) 7/241 (8) 8/250 (9)
9/253 (6) 10/284 (10)

Davidson 30–2–135–5; Meckiff 18–0–129–1; Mackay 3–0–15–0; Benaud 24–3–93–0; Simpson 8–0–25–1; Kline 17.6–6–52–3. *Second innings*—Davidson 24.6–4–87–6; Meckiff 4–1–19–0; Benaud 31–6–69–1; Mackay 21–7–52–1; Kline 4–0–14–0; Simpson 7–2–18–2; O'Neill 1–0–2–0.

Australia

C. C. McDonald c Hunte b Sobers	57	– b Worrell	16
R. B. Simpson b Ramadhin	92	– c sub (L. R. Gibbs) b Hall	0
R. N. Harvey b Valentine	15	– c Sobers b Hall	5
N. C. O'Neill c Valentine b Hall	181	– c Alexander b Hall	26
L. E. Favell run out	45	– c Solomon b Hall	7
K. D. Mackay b Sobers	35	– b Ramadhin	28
A. K. Davidson c Alexander b Hall	44	– run out	80
*R. Benaud lbw b Hall	10	– c Alexander b Hall	52
†A. T. W. Grout lbw b Hall	4	– run out	2
I. Meckiff run out	4	– run out	2
L. F. Kline not out	3	– not out	0
B 2, l-b 8, w 1, n-b 4	15	B 2, l-b 9, n-b 3	14
(130.3 overs)	505	(68.7 overs)	232

1/84 (1) 2/138 (3) 3/194 (2) 4/278 (5)
5/381 (6) 6/469 (7) 7/484 (8) 8/489 (9)
9/496 (10) 10/505 (4)

1/1 (2) 2/7 (3) 3/49 (4) 4/49 (1)
5/57 (5) 6/92 (6) 7/226 (7) 8/228 (8)
9/232 (9) 10/232 (10)

Hall 29.3–1–140–4; Worrell 30–0–93–0; Sobers 32–0–115–2; Valentine 24–6–82–1; Ramadhin 15–1–60–1. *Second innings*—Hall 17.7–3–63–5; Worrell 16–3–41–1; Sobers 8–0–30–0; Valentine 10–4–27–0; Ramadhin 17–3–57–1.

Umpires: C. J. Egar and C. Hoy.

Quite apart from gaining a niche in cricket history as the first Test to end in a tie, this match will always be remembered with enthusiasm because of its excellent cricket. It was played in a most sporting spirit, with the climax coming in a tremendously exciting finish as three wickets fell in the final over.

Australia, set to score 233 runs at a rate of 45 an hour for victory, crumbled before the fiery, sustained pace of Hall, and lost five wickets for 57. The sixth fell at 92. Then the drama began to build up as Davidson, the Australian all-rounder who enjoyed a magnificent match, was joined by Benaud, in a stand which added 134. They were still together half an hour before time, with 27 needed, when Hall took the new ball – a crucial stage.

In the event, however, the West Indies fieldsmen, often at fault during the match, rose to the occasion so that three of the last four batsmen to fall were run out in the desperate race against time. The first run-out came when Benaud called for a sharp single, but Solomon hit the stumps from midwicket to dismiss Davidson. Grout came in and took a single off Sobers, so that when the last momentous over from Hall began, six runs were needed with three wickets left.

The first ball hit Grout on the thigh and a leg-bye resulted; from the second Benaud gave a catch at the wicket as he swung mightily. Meckiff played the third back to the bowler, but when the fourth went through to the wicket-keeper, the batsmen scampered a run. Hall missing a chance to run out Meckiff as the wicketkeeper threw the ball to him. Grout hit the fifth ball high into the air, Hall attempted to take the catch himself, but the ball bounced out, and another run had been gained. Meckiff hit the sixth ball high and to leg, but Hunte cut off the boundary as the batsmen turned for a third run which would have given Australia victory. Hunte threw in superbly, low and fast, and Grout was run out by a foot. So Kline came into face the last two balls with the scores level. He played the seventh ball of the over towards square leg and Meckiff, backing up well, raced down the wicket, only to be out when Solomon again threw down the wicket with only the width of his stump as his target. So ended a match in which both sides had striven throughout for victory with no thought of safety first.

West Indies attacked the bowling from the start of the match only to lose three men for 65 before Sobers, who hit a masterly century in just over two hours, including 15 fours, and Worrell mastered the bowling. Australia succeeded in establishing a lead of 52, largely through the determination of Simpson and O'Neill, who made his highest Test score without reaching his very best form.

West Indies missed several chances at vital times. More fine bowling by Davidson caused West Indies to battle hard for runs in their second innings, and they owed much to some high-class batting from Worrell for their respectable total, swelled usefully on the final morning by a last-wicket stand of 31 between Hall and Valentine.

Australia v West Indies

Second Test Match, at Melbourne, December 30, 1960–January 3, 1961

Australia 348 and 70-3;

West Indies 181 (A. K. Davidson 6-53) and **233** (C. C. Hunte 110).

Australia won by seven wickets.

Benaud: 2 and dnb; 2-58 and 2-49.

A disastrous third day lost West Indies the match. Benaud did Australia good service by winning the toss in excessive heat, but they lost eight wickets for 251 before Mackay and Martin, on his Test debut, added 97. Misson also played his first game for Australia. Martin, chosen mainly for his left-arm slow bowling, made 50 in only 70 minutes.

A crowd of 65,000 saw West Indies follow on 167 behind. Solomon was out hit wicket when his cap fell on the stumps and Hunte alone did anything of real note until Alexander joined him with five men out for 99.

Next morning these two increased their stand to 87, but Australia needed only 67 to win. With Hall bowling at his fastest they lost three wickets for 30 before Simpson and Favell saw them home.

Australia v West Indies

Third Test Match, at Sydney, January 13–18, 1961

West Indies 339 (G. S. Sobers 168; A. K. Davidson 5-80) and **326**

(F. C. M. Alexander 108);

Australia 202 and **241** (L. R. Gibbs 5-66).

West Indies won by 222 runs.

Benaud: 3 and 24; 4-86 and 4-113.

West Indies won by 222 runs thanks mainly to Gibbs, making his first Test appearance in Australia, and Valentine. Most of the Australian batsmen struggled throughout the game against the spin this pair imparted.

Australia were left the mammoth task of scoring 464 to win but the batting by Harvey and O'Neill made a revival possible. Gibbs, however, dispelled their hopes on the fifth morning by taking four wickets for two runs in a spell of 27 balls.

Australia v West Indies

Fourth Test Match, at Adelaide, January 27–February 1, 1961

West Indies 393 (R. B. Kanhai 117; R. Benaud 5-96) and **432-6 dec**

(R. B. Kanhai 115);

Australia 366 (L. R. Gibbs 5-97) and **273-9**.

Drawn.

Benaud: 77 and 17; 5-96 and 2-107.

In a finish almost as exciting as the First Test, a defiant last-wicket partnership prevented West Indies taking the lead in the series. When Kline joined Mackay, an hour and 50 minutes remained with the West Indies total beyond reach. Two minutes later, Sobers, four yards from the bat, appealed confidently for a catch from Mackay off Worrell, but it was turned down by Egar, the umpire, and the pair not only played out time but added 66 runs.

The match was full of incident. Gibbs, the West Indies off-spinner, did the hat-trick in Australia's first innings – the first against Australia this century – and Kanhai scored a hundred in each innings.

West Indies won the toss and after losing Hunte at 12 scored freely on an easy-paced pitch. Benaud kept the score in check with his accurate spin and captured five wickets for 96.

Australia slumped from 281 for five to 281 for eight when Gibbs took a hat-trick. Benaud appeared unperturbed and, receiving unexpected help from Hoare, took the score to 366.

Worrell declared and set Australia to score 460 in just over six and a half hours. Australia lost three wickets for 31 and anxiously faced the last day. All seemed lost until the splendid fighting resistance of Mackay and Kline. For the last over Worrell recalled Hall to bowl to Mackay, but the Queenslander survived.

Australia v West Indies

Fifth Test Match, at Melbourne, February 10–15, 1961

West Indies 292 and **321** (A. K. Davidson 5-84);

Australia 356 (G. S. Sobers 5-120) and **258-8**.

Australia won by two wickets.

Benaud: 3 and 6; 2-55 and 1-53.

When late on the afternoon of February 15, 1961, Valentine spun a ball past batsman and wicketkeeper it was swallowed up by the crowd as they swarmed on to the Melbourne stadium while Mackay and Martin were going through for the winning run. Thus ended an enthralling series which appropriately culminated in excitement and drama.

The beginning matched the end. Though rain fell over the city two days earlier it was generally considered that the side winning the toss would bat first. But Australia had a captain brave in Benaud. With the atmosphere heavy and Hall on the other side, he sent a murmur of surprise round the ground by telling West Indies to take the first innings. In the event, Davidson, the one bowler who, it was hoped, would do most to prove Benaud right, accomplished practically nothing. Instead the spinners worried all except Kanhai and Sobers, and there was no cause for complaint from Australia.

So came the final phase with Australia needing 258 for victory. Simpson began enthusiastically, taking 24 runs off the first ten balls sent down to him, including 18 from the opening over. He was just as convincing when the spinners wrought havoc later and to him more than any other went the main acclaim on this final day of a memorable series.

1961

The impression made by Benaud and Australia against West Indies continued throughout the 1961 Ashes in England. In his Editor's Notes the following year, Norman Preston considered Benaud's impact.

The summer of 1961 brought much satisfaction even if England failed to regain the Ashes from Australia and small attendances at county matches caused alarm. The presence of Richie Benaud and his Australian team contributed to a rekindling of all that is best in cricket. The pattern was set at the end of the previous year at Brisbane where Australia and West Indies played the first tie in the history of Test cricket.

As soon as Benaud arrived in this country, he said his aim was to do away with dull cricket by keeping the game moving and bowling as many overs as possible. He promised there would be no dawdling in the field; the players would move briskly to their positions and in this way keenness and efficiency would be attained. On all controversial issues he and his players intended to leave matters entirely in the hands of the umpires. Benaud proved as good as his word.

Good fellowship and friendliness pervaded the tour and for once the importance of winning a game or a series was not allowed to impinge upon the true spirit of cricket. I have been watching Test cricket for 40 years and I cannot recall a more pleasant atmosphere. I am sure that all cricket-lovers will say: long may it continue.

As for the standard of play in the Tests, both England and Australia have been represented in the past by much stronger sides; yet day after day the struggle was intense, first one side and then the other gaining the upper hand. Surely, there can have been few more dramatic days than the last at Old Trafford, where twice England appeared to have obtained a stranglehold only for Australia to fight back in great style, first with the bat and then with the ball.

ENGLAND 1–2 AUSTRALIA

Norman Preston

Adapting an almost carefree policy throughout their five months' stay in England, the 23rd Australian team to visit this country returned home with their main object achieved. They had won the rubber by victories at Lord's and Old Trafford against one defeat at Headingley and therefore retained the Ashes which they regained during P. B. H. May's MCC tour of the Antipodes in 1958-59. Thirteen years had passed since Australia previously proved victorious in a Test series in England.

The tour was a personal triumph for Richie Benaud, possibly the most popular captain of any overseas team to come to Great Britain. As soon as he arrived Benaud emphasised that he and his men wanted to play attractive cricket wherever they went and that they desired to keep the game moving by bowling as many overs as possible when they were in the field. Moreover, he stressed that, no matter what their opponents did, the Australians would not deviate from their policy of striving for the type of cricket which would please the onlookers.

When the team sailed from Tilbury in September it could be said that they had fulfilled Benaud's promise despite the fact that they had not shown themselves to be immensely strong in either batting or bowling. Their main assets were cheerfulness and boldness, particularly in times of adversity.

They never deliberately set themselves to play for a draw. Benaud preferred to challenge the clock in the three-day matches and, consequently, there were a number of exciting finishes in which the Australians sometimes only narrowly escaped defeat.

Encouraged by Benaud, the Australians never queried an umpire's decision and at times, when they knew they had touched a ball and been caught, did not wait to be given out, but went their way as, indeed, did the England players.

In one respect this was not a happy tour for Benaud. With their refashioned attack which included five bowlers new to English conditions – Ron Gaunt, Frank Misson, Graham McKenzie, Ian Quick and Lindsay Kline, it was clear that the Australians would rely on two key bowlers, Alan Davidson and Benaud. During the first match at Worcester, Benaud broke down with an inflamed tendon in his right shoulder. For many weeks he underwent specialist treatment, and though he did bowl with effect at Old Trafford and on other matches during the latter stages of the tour, he suffered much pain which prevented him exploiting the leg-break or his most deadly delivery, the googly.

Instead, he relied on slow to medium-pace in-and-outswingers, using the seam of the ball to obtain movement. At Old Trafford he bowled round the wicket, and relied on the worn bowlers' footholds to turn the ball. Even then, after only a few overs, the pain returned.

England v Australia

First Test Match, at Birmingham, June 8–13, 1961

England 195 and **401-4** (E. R. Dexter 180, R. Subba Row 112);

Australia 516-9 dec (R. N. Harvey 114).

Drawn.

Benaud: 36*; 3-15 and 0-67.

Australia held the initiative for most of the match, but both sides proved weak in bowling and on the last day England, having faced a first-innings deficit of 321 runs, effected a recovery similar to the one they achieved on the same ground in 1957 when West Indies put them out on the opening day for 186.

Australia had their worries. Benaud, the captain, was a doubtful starter because of a damaged tendon in his right shoulder and O'Neill, like Dexter, was bothered with an injured knee. Yet, apart from Benaud, the invalids acquitted themselves splendidly.

Benaud batted well but when he was wanted most as a bowler on the last day, the pain was so severe he sent down only nine overs. If Benaud had been properly fit it might have been a very different story.

Benaud's shoulder problem kept him out of the Second Test at Lord's, which Australia, captained by Neil Harvey, won by five wickets.

England v Australia
Third Test Match, at Leeds, July 6–8, 1961
Australia 237 (F. S. Trueman 5-58) and **120** (F. S. Trueman 6-30);
England 299 (A. K. Davidson 5-63) and **62-2.**
England won by eight wickets.
Benaud: 0 and 0; 1-86 and 1-22.

England won by eight wickets with two days to spare. This will be remembered as Trueman's Match. Two devastating spells by him caused Australia to collapse. The first occurred immediately after tea on the first day when Australia had reached 183 for two wickets. Then, in the course of six overs, he dismissed five men for 16 runs.

His figures were even more remarkable when he came on at 3.40pm on Saturday with Australia 98 for two. At once he conceded a single to O'Neill before he again claimed five wickets, this time in 24 deliveries, for 0. Trueman finished the match with 11 wickets for 88 runs, easily his best in Test cricket.

Undoubtedly it was this inspired spell by Trueman on the first day which really decided the match. In 90 minutes after tea England captured the remaining eight Australian wickets for the addition of only 54 runs to the interval score.

England resumed on Saturday morning four runs ahead with six wickets standing. They had fought with great tenacity but Dexter, Barrington and Murray rather overdid their caution on this third day. The first half-hour yielded only a single against Davidson (leg-cutters) and Benaud. The two ace Australian bowlers sent down 11 successive maiden overs, but for all his patience Dexter was bowled leg stump, having occupied over two hours for 28.

Trueman tried to take the offensive but after one powerful drive, Burge held him in the same over on the boundary. Australia were on top, but Lock launched a severe attack on Benaud while Murray offered the dead bat to Davidson. In 17 glorious minutes Lock smote Benaud seven times to the boundary, scoring 30 off the Australian captain in three overs. The ball went in all directions but only one four over slip was the outcome of a false stroke. It was impossible to set a field to quieten him.

The arrears were cleared for the loss of two wickets. Then at 98 Trueman returned. He began with his full run and his third ball found Harvey playing too soon. Trueman compelled the batsmen to play at every ball. He bowled Benaud for a pair, and in 35 minutes to tea the score changed to 109 for eight wickets. Trueman's exact analysis from the moment he went on at 98 read 7.5–4–5–6.

England v Australia

Fourth Test Match, at Manchester, July 27–August 1, 1961

Australia won by 54 runs.

Australia

W. M. Lawry lbw b Statham	74	– c Trueman b Allen	102
R. B. Simpson c Murray b Statham	4	– c Murray b Flavell	51
R. N. Harvey c Subba Row b Statham	19	– c Murray b Dexter	35
N. C. O'Neill hit wkt b Trueman	11	– c Murray b Statham	67
P. J. P. Burge b Flavell	15	– c Murray b Dexter	23
B. C. Booth c Close b Statham	46	– lbw b Dexter	9
K. D. Mackay c Murray b Statham	11	– c Close b Allen	18
A. K. Davidson c Barrington b Dexter	0	– not out	77
*R. Benaud b Dexter	2	– lbw b Allen	1
†A. T. W. Grout c Murray b Dexter	2	– c Statham b Allen	0
G. D. McKenzie not out	1	– b Flavell	32
B 4, l-b 1	5	B 6, l-b 9, w 2	17
(63.4 overs)	190	(171.4 overs)	432

1/8 (2) 2/51 (3) 3/89 (4) 4/106 (5)
5/150 (1) 6/174 (7) 7/185 (6) 8/185 (8)
9/189 (10) 10/190 (9)

1/113 (2) 2/175 (3) 3/210 (1) 4/274 (5)
5/290 (4) 6/296 (6) 7/332 (7) 8/334 (9)
9/334 (10) 10/432 (11)

Trueman 14–1–55–1; Statham 21–3–53–5; Flavell 22–8–61–1; Dexter 6.4–2–16–3. *Second innings*—Trueman 32–6–92–0; Statham 44–9–106–1; Flavell 29.4–4–65–2; Allen 38–25–58–4; Dexter 20–4–61–3; Close 8–1–33–0.

England

G. Pullar b Davidson	63	– c O'Neill b Davidson	26
R. Subba Row c Simpson b Davidson	2	– b Benaud	49
E. R. Dexter c Davidson b McKenzie	16	– c Grout b Benaud	76
*P. B. H. May c Simpson b Davidson	95	– b Benaud	0
D. B. Close lbw b McKenzie	33	– c O'Neill b Benaud	8
K. F. Barrington c O'Neill b Simpson	78	– lbw b Mackay	5
†J. T. Murray c Grout b Mackay	24	– c Simpson b Benaud	4
D. A. Allen c Booth b Simpson	42	– c Simpson b Benaud	10
F. S. Trueman c Harvey b Simpson	3	– c Benaud b Simpson	8
J. B. Statham c Mackay b Simpson	4	– b Davidson	8
J. A. Flavell not out	0	– not out	0
B 2, l-b 4, w 1	7	B 5, w 2	7
(163.4 overs)	367	(71.4 overs)	201

1/3 (2) 2/43 (3) 3/154 (1) 4/212 (4)
5/212 (5) 6/272 (7) 7/358 (6) 8/362 (8)
9/367 (9) 10/367 (10)

1/40 (1) 2/150 (3) 3/150 (4) 4/158 (5)
5/163 (2) 6/171 (7) 7/171 (6) 8/189 (8)
9/193 (9) 10/201 (10)

Davidson 39–11–70–3; McKenzie 38–11–106–2; Mackay 40–9–81–1; Benaud 35–15–80–0; Simpson 11.4–4–23–4. *Second innings*—Davidson 14.4–1–50–2; McKenzie 4–1–20–0; Benaud 32–11–70–6; Simpson 8–4–21–1; Mackay 13–7–33–1.

Umpires: J. G. Langridge and W. E. Phillipson.

Australia won by 54 runs and made certain of retaining the Ashes. They deserved great credit for fighting back three times when in difficulties, but England, on top for a large part of the match, disappointed, particularly on the last day.

Dropped catches proved costly to England and had an important bearing on the result. The game was intensely keen throughout and was the best of the series.

Australia cleared their deficit for the loss of two wickets, but England steadily captured wickets. On the last morning Australia lost three men while adding three runs and the total went from 331 for six to 334 for nine. Allen took all three without cost in 15 balls.

At that point Australia were only 157 on and England looked to have the game comfortably won, but there developed a splendid last-wicket stand between Davidson and McKenzie. Davidson took 20 in an over off Allen, and removed his menace on a pitch taking a fair amount of spin. The other bowlers could make no impression and 98 were added before the innings closed. It was Australia's highest last-wicket Test stand in England. This not only made England's task harder in terms of runs, but it took valuable time away from them. They were set to get 256 in three hours, 50 minutes.

Pullar and Subba Row began with a brisk partnership of 40. Then came a glorious display of controlled hitting by Dexter which put England right up with the clock. Driving with tremendous power and cutting and hooking splendidly, Dexter took only 84 minutes to score 76, which included one six and 14 fours. The second-wicket stand with Subba Row produced 110 in that time.

Suddenly the position changed completely. Benaud, bowling round the wicket and pitching into the rough of Trueman's footholds, brought such a collapse that in 20 minutes to tea England virtually lost the game. After getting Dexter caught at the wicket, Benaud bowled May round his legs, had Close, following one drive for six, caught at backward square leg, and bowled the solid Subba Row.

England resumed after tea needing 93 in 85 minutes with only Barrington of their leading batsmen left. When Murray and Barrington fell for the addition of eight all thoughts of an England victory had gone, and it became only a question of whether Australia could finish the match in time. They did so with 20 minutes to spare and thus Australia gained their first Test win at Old Trafford since 1902. Benaud claimed six for 70, his best performance against England. Owing to his shoulder trouble he attempted little spin, being content to let the ball do its work on dropping into the rough.

England v Australia
Fifth Test Match, at The Oval, August 17–22, 1961
England 256 and **370-8** (R. Subba Row 137, K. D. Mackay 5-121);
Australia 494 (P. J. P. Burge 181, N. C. O'Neill 117).
Drawn.
Benaud: 6; 1-35 and 3-113.

Although the destination of the Ashes had already been decided in Australia's favour, victory in this match would have enabled England to draw the rubber. Instead, England made such a poor start that they always seemed to be fighting against adversity.

There was a rare duel between the rival captains, May and Benaud. It lasted over half an hour. May appeared to be the master and produced some superb strokes, lifting Benaud straight into the vacant deep until, trying to force him over mid-on, he skyed the ball to deep point where Lawry was waiting for the catch.

The crowd cheered Benaud all the way to the wicket and though the later batsmen, apart from Grout, caused little trouble, Burge maintained his onslaught until he was ninth to leave, having hit 22 fours in his 181 which took six hours and 50 minutes. Australia held a lead of 238.

1961–62

There were no Test matches in the Australian summer. New South Wales won their ninth consecutive Sheffield Shield, and Benaud added 255 for the seventh wicket against Victoria with Grahame Thomas. It remains a Sheffield Shield record.

An animated first day, in which New South Wales made 398 for eight wickets, was marked by a record seventh-wicket partnership of 255 runs by Thomas and Benaud, after the sixth wicket had fallen at 141. Benaud, resolute and aggressive, contributed 140 (two sixes, 17 fours) in three hours; Thomas, brilliant after an early struggle, was 119 not out when Benaud declared at the end of the day. Benaud's attacking policy was cheered by 13,000 people, and he received an ovation after being caught on the boundary.

1962–63

AUSTRALIA 1–1 ENGLAND   Leslie Smith

England went to Australia in 1962-63 with two main objectives: to regain the Ashes; and to provide cricket capable of recapturing the enthusiasm of the public, as West Indies did two years earlier.

They achieved neither, but in each case the margin between success and failure was so narrow that the tour could well have gone down as one of the most interesting for many years.

Unfortunately, when everything seemed set for a thrilling climax, things began to go wrong, and in the end everyone felt there had been a big let-down which tended to obscure all that had gone before.

Although somewhat tarnished by previous events, the reputations of Benaud and Dexter as enterprising captains were still reasonably intact. As it happened this final game turned out to be the dullest and by far the worst of the five.

During the acclimatisation period in Perth, Dexter often promised attacking cricket at receptions and press conferences, and in the majority of the games this policy was carried out. Benaud, too, declared his intention of seeing that his players would adopt positive methods. All this was forgotten in the Tests where victory, or rather the avoidance of defeat, became the all-important factor.

Benaud began with a flourish, taking seven for 18 with some remarkable bowling for New South Wales and following with six for 115 in the first innings of the Brisbane Test. He looked to be England's biggest problem at that point; but he fell away badly, and his 17 Test wickets cost over 40 runs each.

As a captain he retained his enthusiasm and rarely allowed the game to settle into a routine, but he appeared to become more cautious than in the past, and at Adelaide, in particular, he gave up hope far too soon.

Before the Test series, Benaud took his best first-class figures against the tourists.

MCC were outplayed and New South Wales became the first State side to beat an English team by an innings since 1883. Benaud declared at lunchtime on the third day 184 ahead. Then he mesmerised the MCC batsmen with a remarkable spell of controlled leg-breaks, only nine scoring strokes being made off him in an analysis of 18.1–10–18–7. The innings lasted under three hours.

Australia v England

First Test Match, at Brisbane, November 30–December 5, 1962

Australia 404 (B. C. Booth 112) and **362-4 dec;**

England 389 (R. Benaud 6-115) and **278-6.**

Drawn.

Benaud: 51 and dnb; 6-115 and 1-71.

For the first time in Australia–England matches, a Test at Brisbane failed to produce a definite result. Australia eventually went reasonably close to winning, but England deserved to draw for their good fighting performance.

Australia's last four wickets added 210. Pullar and Sheppard, both missed early, gave England a useful start with 62, but the appearance of Benaud changed the situation. He dismissed both, and although Dexter played a fine innings of 70, including ten fours, in two hours, he also bowled him before the close when England were 169 for four. Benaud finished with six for 115.

Australia v England

Second Test Match, at Melbourne, December 29, 1962–January 3, 1963

Australia 316 and **248** (B. C. Booth 103; F. S. Trueman 5-62);

England 331 (M. C. Cowdrey 113; A. K. Davidson 6-75) and **237-3**

(Rev D. S. Sheppard 113).

England won by seven wickets.

Benaud: 36 and 4; 1-82 and 0-69.

England won with an hour and a quarter to spare after a thrilling struggle throughout. Only on the last day when England won with plenty in hand did one side take command. The rest of the match was a tremendous battle for supremacy with each side gaining and losing the initiative several times.

England thoroughly deserved their first victory in Australia since 1954-55, showing better tactics and more aggression. Only in ground-fielding did Australia match them.

Australia v England

Third Test Match, at Sydney, January 11–15, 1963

England 279 (R. B. Simpson 5-57) and **104** (A. K. Davidson 5-25);
Australia 319 (F. J. Titmus 7-79) and **67-2.**
Australia won by eight wickets.
Benaud: 15 and dnb; 1-60 and 1-29.

Australia won by eight wickets with more than a day and a half remaining. Until England collapsed badly at the start of their second innings the game was fought out evenly and a fine struggle seemed in prospect.

Australia, 40 ahead, virtually won the game when Davidson, in a magnificent spell with the new ball, dismissed Pullar, Dexter and Sheppard in 25 balls. Cowdrey fell to Benaud's first delivery, which lifted, and England were still three behind with four wickets gone. Simpson, who had a fine all-round match, helped in the collapse by holding three successive catches at first slip. Benaud's two wickets enabled him to become the leading Australian wicket-taker, beating Ray Lindwall's 228.

Australia v England

Fourth Test Match, at Adelaide, January 25–30, 1963

Australia 393 (R. N. Harvey 154, N. C. O'Neill 100) and **293;**
England 331 (G. D. McKenzie 5-89) and **223-4** (K. F. Barrington 132*).
Drawn.
Benaud: 16 and 48; 1-82 and 1-38.

Several factors contributed to the stalemate in this match, but to some extent it was due to a fear by either side of losing. Australia's chance of victory virtually disappeared when Davidson broke down with a pulled muscle in his fourth over and could not bowl again in the match. At the end of the fourth day Australia, with four wickets left, led by 287, and Benaud, in the absence of Davidson and on a still perfect pitch, concentrated on saving the game.

He declined a declaration, and when the innings ended just on lunchtime on the last morning England needed 356 at 89 an hour.

Australia v England

Fifth Test Match, at Sydney, February 15–20, 1963

England 321 (K. F. Barrington 101) and **268-8 dec;**

Australia 349 (P. J. P. Burge 103; F. J. Titmus 5-103) and **152-4.**

Drawn.

Benaud: 57 and dnb; 2-71 and 3-71.

The deciding match of the series, far from being the exciting contest expected, turned out to be a dull, lifeless game which did immense harm to cricket, particularly in Australia.

Much of the blame can be traced to the ground, which never allowed the players to show the game at its best, but the players must be held responsible to a fair extent. Little effort was made to overcome the conditions. On most of the days there was a good deal of barracking, and the game ended with booing and slow hand-clapping.

For the first time three matches between the countries in Australia were drawn, and never before, when five games had been played between the countries, was the series undecided.

During the match Trueman and Benaud equalled Alec Bedser's 236 Test wickets, only Statham being ahead of them.

1963–64

AUSTRALIA 1–1 SOUTH AFRICA

South African cricket received a splendid boost by the achievements of the team in Australia during the three and a half months from October 1963 to February 1964. Not only did they share the series, each side winning one game with the three other Tests drawn, but they surprised and delighted everybody by the quality of their play.

The Australians disappointed. The absence of Davidson, who had retired, was a big handicap to the attack, but the batting was expected to be powerful. In fact, only Booth and Lawry justified themselves to the full.

Benaud gave up the captaincy after the First Test and Simpson took over. He had the satisfaction of leading his side to victory in his first game as captain, but thereafter had a difficult task in saving the series.

In what turned out to be Benaud's last Test as Australian captain, the left-arm fast bowler Ian Meckiff was no-balled for throwing in his first over. Benaud did not bowl him again, and Meckiff retired after the match.

Australia v South Africa
First Test Match, at Brisbane, December 6–11, 1963
Australia 435 (B. C. Booth 169; P. M. Pollock 6-95) and **144-1 dec;**
South Africa 346 (E. J. Barlow 114; R. Benaud 5-68) and **13-1.**
Drawn.
Benaud: 43 and dnb; 5-68 and 0-4.

There was never much hope of a definite result with one day lost through rain, but the match was made memorable by the no-balling of Meckiff for throwing and his subsequent retirement from first-class cricket.

Meckiff was no-balled by Egar on his second, third, fifth and ninth deliveries. That was his only over. Egar was booed and Meckiff was carried shoulder-high by a section of the crowd at the close.

South Africa made a promising start, but ran into trouble against Benaud and were 157 for four at the end of the second day.

No play was possible on Monday, and on the fourth day extra police were sent to the ground because of fears that the umpires, selectors and Benaud might be molested because of the Meckiff incident. There were no scenes.

Benaud missed the Second Test, which Australia won by eight wickets, because of injury. Bobby Simpson stood in as captain; Benaud – who had announced his plan to retire at the end of the season – suggested the selectors look to the future and keep Simpson as captain.

Australia v South Africa
Third Test Match, at Sydney, January 10–15, 1964
Australia 260 (P. M. Pollock 5-83) and **450-9 dec** (J. T. Partridge 5-123);
South Africa 302 (R. G. Pollock 122) and **326-5;**
Drawn.
Benaud: 43 and 90; 3-55 and 0-61.

A game of many highlights began with bowlers encouraged by a pitch generous in grass, but ended with batsmen once more entrenched on a friendly strip.

Benaud and McKenzie completed Australia's recovery with an attractive partnership of 160, which fell only five short of the Australian seventh-wicket record set up by Hill and Trumble 66 years earlier.

So South Africa went in a second time needing 409 in seven and a quarter hours, and the fact that they got to within 83 of that figure with five wickets left showed how the nature of the pitch changed.

Benaud then played his last Sheffield Shield game at Sydney, against South Australia.

Richie Benaud, in his farewell Shield match, played a valuable and beautifully controlled innings for 118; in the second innings he engaged in a century stand with young Walters.

Australia v South Africa
Fourth Test Match, at Adelaide, January 24–29, 1964
Australia 345 (T. L. Goddard 5-60) and **331;**
South Africa 595 (E. J. Barlow 201, R. G. Pollock 175, N. J. N. Hawke 6-139)
and **82-0.**
South Africa won by ten wickets.
Benaud: 7 and 34; 0-101 and 0-17.

South Africa won by ten wickets, so bringing the series level at 1–1 with one to play. They gained this well-deserved victory with cricket much more lively in character and of a higher standard than that of the Australians.

Before his final Test, Benaud played his last Shield game, making 76 and 120 not out against South Australia at Adelaide. He also took five wickets in the match, a thriller that

NSW won by six runs. Three days later, he began his farewell Test appearance.

Australia v South Africa

Fifth Test Match, at Sydney, February 7–12, 1964

Australia 311 (B. C. Booth 102*; J. T. Partridge 7-91) and **270;**

South Africa 411 (K. C. Bland 126) and **76-0.**

Drawn.

Benaud: 11 and 3; 4-118 and 0-25.

The careful play of both sides reflected the fact that the series depended on this match. When the last ball had been bowled, Australia were probably grateful that progress had been so tardy, for otherwise the rubber might well have gone against them.

South Africa were left to score 171 to win but, having been held up by a last-wicket stand of 45 in an hour and a quarter, they had only 85 minutes in which to get the runs.

Benaud finished with 63 Tests, 2,201 runs at 24.45 and 248 wickets – then an Australian record – at 27.03. At the age of 33, it was time to say goodbye.

At the close of the first-class programme Richie Benaud joined former colleagues R. N. Harvey and A. K. Davidson in retirement. After leading New South Wales in the first two Shield matches, Benaud advised the State selectors of his intention to retire at the end of the season and of his readiness to relinquish the leadership. The selectors appointed Bobby Simpson to succeed Benaud as captain. Benaud had similarly stepped down from the Test captaincy after missing the Second Test through injury.

Benaud had led Australia since 1958, and during his period Australia did not lose a Test rubber. The NSW Cricket Association, in recording appreciation of Benaud's services, said: "His bowling and batting performances speak for themselves. His success as captain was due not only to his exceptional cricketing prowess and his profound knowledge, but also to his natural ability in the leadership of men."

Benaud's Career
in Statistics

Batting

	M	I	NO	R	HS	100	50	Avge	Ct
Tests	63	97	7	2201	122	3	9	24.45	65
First-class	259	365	44	11719	187	23	61	36.50	254

Bowling

	M	Balls	Runs	Wkts	BB	5	10	Avge
Tests	63	19108	6704	248	7–72	16	1	27.03
First-class	259	60445	23370	945	7–18	56	9	24.73

Test Record

Overall
P63 W24 L13 D25 T1

As captain
P28 W12 L4 D11 T1
Australia won five and lost none of the seven series in which Benaud was
captain.

BY COUNTRY

	M	Runs	HS	100s	Avge	Wkts	BB	5/10	Avge	Ct
v England	27	767	97	0	19.66	83	6–70	4/0	31.81	32
v India	8	144	25	0	14.40	52	7–72	5/1	18.38	5
v Pakistan	4	144	56	0	28.80	19	5–93	1/0	21.89	2
v South Africa	13	684	122	2	36.00	52	5–49	5/0	27.17	15
v West Indies	11	462	121	1	27.17	42	5–96	1/0	30.42	11
Home	29	1078	90	0	23.95	104	6–115	5/0	30.74	33
Away	34	1123	122	3	24.95	144	7–72	11/1	24.35	32

FIRST-CLASS RECORD, SEASON BY SEASON

	M	Runs	HS	100s	Avge	Wkts	BB	5/10	Avge	Ct
1948–49	1	2	2	0	2.00		did not bowl			0
1949–50	5	250	93	0	31.25	5	2–71	0/0	54.00	2
1950–51	5	184	55	0	36.80	11	4–93	0/0	34.63	6
1951–52	9	426	117	1	30.42	14	3–111	0/0	50.07	10
1952–53	13	734	167*	2	43.17	38	5–87	1/0	31.73	14
1953	22	748	135	1	27.70	57	7–46	2/0	22.33	18
1953–54	8	811	158	3	62.38	35	5–33	2/0	30.54	11
1954–55	20	976	125	2	34.86	42	4–15	0/0	38.93	22
1955–56	10	587	103*	2	41.92	44	6–76	2/0	21.61	10
1956	23	871	160	1	34.84	60	6–31	3/1	22.28	14
1956–57	18	984	113	1	41.00	94	7–72	6/1	21.10	18
1957–58	18	817	187	4	51.06	106	7–46	11/2	19.39	18
1958–59	13	426	76	0	28.40	82	7–32	6/1	19.25	17
1959–60	11	279	54	0	23.25	65	6–74	5/1	19.95	9
1960–61	14	588	119	1	34.59	53	5–31	2/0	27.55	10
1961	22	627	80*	0	25.08	61	6–70	5/0	23.54	18
1961–62	13	634	140	1	42.27	72	5–30	6/1	18.67	18
1962–63	18	832	135	1	37.82	67	7–18	3/2	30.13	24
1963–64	11	956	132	3	56.24	29	5–68	1/0	41.17	11
1967–68	5	287	89	0	47.83	10	5–29	1/0	17.90	4

TEST HUNDREDS AND FIVE-WICKET HAULS

121 v West Indies, at Kingston, Jamaica, 1954–55

122 v South Africa at Johannesburg, 1957–58

100 v South Africa at Johannesburg, 1957–58

7–72 v India at Madras (now Chennai), 1956–57

6–52 v India at Calcutta (now Kolkata), 1956–57

5–53 v India at Calcutta (now Kolkata), 1956–57

5–49 v South Africa at Cape Town, 1957–58

5–114 v South Africa at Durban, 1957–58

5–84 v South Africa at Johannesburg, 1957–58

5–82 v South Africa at Port Elizabeth, 1957–58

5–83 v England at Sydney, 1958–59

5–91 v England at Adelaide, 1958–59

5–93 v Pakistan at Karachi, 1959–60

5–76 v India at Delhi, 1959–60

5–43 v India at Madras (now Chennai), 1959–60

5–96 v West Indies at Adelaide, 1960–61

6–70 v England at Manchester, 1961

6–115 v England at Brisbane, 1962–63

5–68 v South Africa at Brisbane, 1963–64

Acknowledgements

Benaud in Wisden would not have been possible without the expertise, enthusiasm and patience of a number of people. That's especially true of Charlotte Atyeo and Holly Jarrald at Bloomsbury and everyone at Wisden, particularly Christopher Lane, Hugh Chevallier and Steven Lynch.

I'm extremely grateful to all the writers who were happy for their work to be reprinted: Jonathan Agnew, E. J. Brack, Tim de Lisle, Gideon Haigh, Emma John, Quentin Letts, Tony Lewis, Dr Greg Manning, Andrew Miller, Sam Peters, Dileep Premachandran and Christian Ryan. I'd also like to thank Charles Barr for his expert proofreading, Rob Bagchi, Cris Freddi and Scott Murray for their advice, and Jay Jennings and Royal Jennings for their love and encouragement.

Most of all I'd like to thank Alan Davidson for his lovely foreword, and Daphne Benaud for her unfailingly generous support of the book. And of course Richie Benaud, for providing the soundtrack to some of the happiest moments of my life.